THE NEWSPAPER THAT SCOOPED THE WORLD

The Cologne Post and British journalism in the occupied Rhineland 1919-1929

James Stewart and
Rob Campbell

Copyright © 2020 James Stewart and Rob Campbell

All rights reserved

No part of this book may be reproduced, or stored in a retrieval system, or transmitted in any form or by any means, electronic, mechanical, photocopying, recording, or otherwise, without express written permission of the publisher.

Cover design by Wil Stewart

Illustrations from the authors' private collection: cover image of the Watch on the Rhine from the 1919 Christmas souvenir number of the Cologne Post and illustrations from the paper of 3 April 1919.

ISBN: 9798602841404

1234567

Dedicated to the memory of Cpl. Evan Jenkin Kingsbury (1889-1981) who marched from Ypres to Cologne after the Armistice in 1918 and served for a year with the Army of Occupation in the Rhineland

The Cologne Post

A Daily Paper published by the Army of the Rhine.

No 4. COLOGNE, Thursday, April 3, 1919. Price 20 Pfg.

CAPTAIN FRYATT'S MURDER GERMAN INQUIRY OPENED

POST OFFICE WAGES RAISED

TERRITORIALS TO TOUR TOWN

BATTLE WITH SPARTACISTS AT FRANKFORT

MURDER OF CAPTAIN FRYATT.

GERMAN INQUIRY OPENS

POST OFFICE WAGES UP.

ARBITRATORS AWARD.

TERRITORIALS TO TOUR THE TOWNS.

LEAGUE OF NATIONS.

JAPANESE OPINION.

VISITS TO THE BATTLEFIELDS

CONFLICT IN KOREA.

BOLSHEVIST DEFEAT NEAR KIEV.

PASSED TO YOU, PLEASE

MILITARY STAFF COLLEGE.

RE-OPENED

QUESTIONS IN THE COMMONS.

INTERESTING POINTS RAISED

PRISONERS' SWORDS.

OFFICERS' DEMOBILISATION.

TERRITORIALS IN INDIA.

OVERSEAS TROOPS.

ARMY OF OCCUPATION POLICY.

LOOK AT YOUR MONEY.

VERY DOUBTFUL PERSONS.

TO PAY FOR FOOD.

TAX ON BACHELORS

DISCUSSION OF SEX PROBLEMS.

ARCHBISHOPS VIEWS.

CANADIANS IN BRUSSELS.

WANTED! TWO SOLDIERS

OFFICER DECAPITATED

WILSON'S REGRETS.

HOW DID THEY ESCAPE?

DUSSELDORF SOCIALISTS.

STRIKES AND STRIKERS.

ENGLAND

GERMANY

CENTRAL CRIMINAL COURT.

TWENTY-TWO BIGAMISTS

"DON'T PITY, FIND HIM A JOB." WELL DONE, BROTHERHOOD

BLOCKADE OF GERMANY

TRANSPORT SUNK.

MAY DAY — PEACE DAY.

THE ORIENT EXPRESS

CONTENTS

Title Page

Copyright

Dedication

Introduction   1

1. 'The greatest scoop journalism has ever known'   7

2. 'A British newspaper for the Britons in Rhineland'   14

3. Journalists in Uniform   28

4. What's in Today's Paper?   37

5. 'Germany should be taught her lesson'   47

6. Home on the Rhine   69

7. The Editor's Letterbox   84

8. 'The Greater Game'   104

9. Informing, educating & entertaining   115

Map of the occupied Rhineland 1919   129

References   130

Notes   137

Introduction

When the guns fell silent on the Western Front on 11 November 1918, the defeated German army went home. British soldiers, just as eager to get out of uniform, were ordered to remain on a war footing. Two hundred and seventy thousand of them soon discovered that they were to march 200 miles to the Rhine, following the retreating Germans. In early December, they joined French, Belgian and American troops in occupying the whole of the Rhineland west of the river, along with bridgeheads on the eastern bank. The British army of occupation had its headquarters in the historic city of Cologne, capital of the Rhineland. It was there that a unique newspaper, the Cologne Post was founded and published, to serve the soldiers and a wider British readership in Germany for more than 10 years.

In 1919, the British on the Rhine were cut off from information. In the early years of the occupation, it took two days for newspapers to reach Cologne from London. At a time of continuing turmoil and uncertainty in the world, the troops in Germany were in the dark. The Cologne Post set out to enlighten them. They did not need information about military matters in the Rhineland – they got that efficiently through the Army's own channels. What the Post gave them was up-to-date news from home – whether that was politics, crime, scandal or sport. It told them about the world 'on their doorsteps', including 'what to see, where and when to see it and what it will cost.' Crucially, it also shaped their view of that world and their place in it.

The years during which the Cologne Post was published saw the creation of the BBC, with its aim to 'inform, educate and entertain'. That phrase encapsulates much of the mission of the paper. Throughout the occupation, the newspaper – whatever the constraints – avoided becoming a mouthpiece for the military authorities. Indeed, it was proud to claim that it defied the military authorities to publish the terms of the Peace Treaty with Germany before any other newspaper.

As well as news from Britain, Germany, the Empire and the wider world, the Post promoted education, encouraging literacy and self-improvement. It published serialisations of stories and information about opportunities for entertainment and recreation. In the early months, its letters column provided a forum for the British in Germany to discuss issues of concern and debate the terms of engagement with the occupied population.

Until the Treaty of Versailles was signed in June 1919, a quarter of a million British soldiers remained on a war footing in and around Cologne. It was the Peace Treaty which gave the Post its greatest claim to fame – as the first newspaper in the world to publish the terms which the Allies would impose on Germany. The paper revealed the details to its readers in Germany before they had reached the German government in Berlin. How it pulled off what it called 'the greatest scoop in the history of journalism' is a fascinating episode in the story of this unique newspaper.

At the heart of that story was the team of journalists drawn from the ranks of the Army to produce a highly professional daily paper in difficult circumstances. Just one of their many challenges was the fact that the German newspaper on whose presses the Post was printed did not have typesetting machines which could handle English; neither could any of their compositors read the language.

Once peace had been agreed, the nature of the occupation and the make-up of the occupying army changed. The paper responded to its changing readership, introducing a regular column for women once army wives were allowed to come to Cologne. Later, there would be regular features for children too. In the early years, letters to the editor regularly raised questions about relations between men and women. Some criticised, while others defended, 'fraternization' with German women. Female members of the occupying army complained about the attitude of their male compatriots. Tommy bemoaned the lack of interest – or the 'modern' attitudes – of women at home when he encountered them on leave. The Editor's Letterbox was a forum to air and debate this and many other issues of concern to the British colony in Cologne.

The paper relied on wire services and supportive journalists for its coverage of events in Britain, the Empire and the wider world. But its own reporting on Cologne and the rest of the Rhineland throws a light on life in Germany during a tumultuous period in its history. While civilian administration continued in the occupied zone and representatives from the Rhineland took their seats in the Reichstag in Berlin, the ordinances of the Inter Allied High Commission gave extensive powers to the military over the occupied population. The Post's reports on cases brought before the British Summary Court range from insults to the wives of His Brittanic Majesty's Forces to serious breaches of the regulations governing political meetings - especially those of a revolutionary flavour.

The Post had occasion to defend the reputation of the Rhine Army against allegations in the London press that soldiers' teams were regularly meeting Germans on the sports field. There is no evidence of such matches in the pages it devoted to sport. As a large broadsheet, it gave over one of its four daily pages to reports of inter-army fixtures in the Rhineland as well as extensive coverage of soccer, rugby, racing and other sports at home. There may have been wide disparities in the social and sporting backgrounds of the officers and other ranks, but the sports pages had something for all of them. And the paper's focus on sport reflected the army's emphasis on physical activity to keep its young soldiers occupied and to discharge their energy.

In its early days, questions were asked in the House of Commons about the Post's policy of accepting advertising from German businesses. The editor took a robust and professional line, arguing that serving his readers by informing them of services they might want and need was a fundamental part of a paper's remit. Advertising played an important part in the Post's finances and it would publish extensive supplements linked to special events, such as the Cologne Trade Fair. Just as important was information for British businesses – part of a wider expatriate community – about opportunities in the occupied territories and the rest of Germany.

The last issue of the Cologne Post & Wiesbaden Times (as it had become) appeared on 3 November 1929, shortly before the final British withdrawal from the Rhine. The last British representative – the High Commissioner in the Inter-Allied Rhineland High Commission – left when France pulled its forces out on 30 June 1930.

Six years later German troops crossed the Rhine in breach of the Versailles Treaty of 1919 and the Locarno Treaties of 1925. The reoccupation of the Rhineland was the first of Hitler's moves to regain territories lost by Germany in 1918 and the first of the Nazi regime's breaches of international treaties to be met with appeasement. Just 15 years later, British soldiers would be back in Germany, this time as occupiers of a dismembered state forced to surrender unconditionally.

The British in Germany after 1945 could rely on the BBC and the British Forces Broadcasting Service for news of home and the wider world. For their predecessors in the original Rhine Army, the Cologne Post was the only source of up-to-date news and information.

This book tells the story of the paper and its people –

those who produced it and those who read it. The time and the place meant that this was a unique publication – an English-language newspaper published in a great German city. Cologne, under its Mayor Konrad Adenauer, was both part of - yet cut off from - the country whose direction would decide the future of Europe. This is the story of a bold and innovative venture in the history of journalism and the way a newspaper shaped – and was shaped by – its unique community.

1. 'The Greatest Scoop Journalism Has Ever Known'

On 7 May 1919, Germany's high representatives were summoned to the Trianon Palace at Versailles to receive the text of the draft Peace Treaty which would be imposed upon them by the victorious Allies. The Armistice of 11 November 1918 had brought four years of slaughter to an end, but until peace was agreed, the war would not be over.

It was 3pm when the German delegation entered the Hall of Mirrors to receive their copy of the 200-page draft treaty. Only hours later, the Cologne Post was the first newspaper in the world to publish a detailed account of what the draft contained. A special edition was on the streets of a German city before midnight. Not until the next morning would the terms reach the government in Berlin.[1]

On several occasions in its 10-year history, the paper looked back on that day, claiming it as 'the greatest scoop journalism has ever known' and 'the biggest scoop in the history of newspaper effort'. Viewed from an age of instant news and social media, it is hard to appreciate why journalists a hundred years ago should have been so proud of their achievement. But in the days before radio, news was a physical commodity, which took time to produce – it had to be set in type, printed and distributed. For the staff of the Post, the 'scoop' was the 'supreme satisfaction, which only newspaper men can thoroughly appreciate'.

The story of the scoop became the founding legend of the paper, not simply because it was a competitive triumph. It was celebrated and revisited because – the paper claimed – the scoop involved publishing the news of the peace treaty in defiance of the state, in the form of a military order in a time of war. Just how serious an offence that defiance was, cannot be known. It is possible that someone, somewhere, turned a blind eye. But what is clear is that the newspaper – as an institution – was inordinately proud of its story – that it put its duty to publish, to inform its readers, ahead of any narrower, military duty.

In its first anniversary edition on 31 March 1920, the Post published an account of how it pulled off its coup. Arrangements had been made for the terms of the treaty to be telegraphed from Paris as soon as they were released to the Press. But the paper stole a march on the competition. In 1920, it was still coy about the details: 'Just how it was accomplished is an interesting story that may not yet be revealed.'

In his memoir of the occupation, Ferdinand Tuohy – who clearly knew the Cologne Post well – revealed the inside story as it had been told to him. Quoting William Le Crerar, the only original member of staff to be with the Post to the end, he describes how a copy of the treaty was flown from Paris and brought to the office in Cologne by a courier with an armed motorcycle escort.

> A guard of men with fixed bayonets stood at every entrance, and no-one was allowed to leave or come into the building until the machines began printing. The only person allowed, as a necessary exception, to enter the building was a messenger who handed a telegram to Mr. Nevill, the Acting-Editor. Nevill opened it, read it, and put it in his pocket, and it was not until the papers were actually on the streets that he showed the staff the telegram. It was an order to hold up the publication of the Treaty. 'I don't care if they hang me for it,' said Nevill. 'We've got the greatest scoop ever known.' [2]

How the Post got hold of a copy of the treaty before its general release is not known. Years later, in a tribute to J. W. Nevill, it remained coy about the details but recalled his 'lapsus mentis' (slip of mind), which bypassed the interdiction and secured the scoop:

> Everything had been carefully planned for that dramatic coup and the plans were within an ace of fruition when a wire came. What that wire contained, who opened it, and who so far forgot to mention its 'verboten' contents until the edition was on sale, can be guessed. [3]

Within an hour of receiving the document, Cologne had been 'smothered' with posters advertising the special edition. Outlying Army units were alerted by telephone. The doors of the composing room were locked and within four hours, the story was set and printed. By 'middle evening' the courtyard outside the printing works was 'a mass of excited humanity'.

The special edition carried what was, for those days, a huge headline across all five columns: 'The draft Treaty of Peace "For the prevention of wars in the future and for the betterment of mankind"'. The first column made clear that this was a summary of the draft terms, which were laid out under fifteen separate headings. Those waiting outside the print works in Cologne would be the first in the world, apart from those directly involved in Versailles, to know what Germany was being forced to accept.

> Staff officers, German officials, newsvendors, men and women of every station in life waiting with undisguised anxiety to know the price demanded – take it or leave it – for having sought arbitrament by the sword. They read their Fate in the Cologne Post, which acting as the mouthpiece of the Allies, was something much greater than a mere newspaper which had brought off a world's record. [4]

The German delegation at Versailles had travelled to France on 28 April and been kept waiting for more than a week while the Allies rushed to complete the draft of the treaty. It was only in the early hours of 7 May that Allied officials had received their own copies of the 75,000-word document – and many of them were appalled at its harshness. The German were given only one copy – in English and French – and worked through the night to translate it and send mimeographed copies of the translation to Berlin.[5] Before it reached the German Government, the summary had been published in Cologne.

The special edition had been printed and the regular daily paper was running on the presses by the time the officially released summary of the treaty reached the paper. By then, the Cologne Post's staff had retired to celebrate their scoop at a bar in the city frequented by local journalists. As they entered, 'the high note of excited conversation ceased abruptly and dead silence ensued'.

> The only sound in the salon was of our glasses being filled. We stood and said 'Prosit' to them and 'cheerio' to each other. Then one came across, offered his hand and said in a broken voice: 'Our colonies and our ships'. We left at once, being bowed out with punctilious politeness ... [6]

Under the terms of the draft treaty, Germany was to lose all its colonies, its merchant navy, one third of its coalfields, three-quarters of its iron ore deposits and one third of its blast furnaces. Its army and navy were to be reduced to 'pitiful proportions' and the level of reparations was still to be set.[7] John Maynard Keynes who was part of the British delegation, described the terms as an unbearably harsh 'Carthaginian Peace'.

Among the Allies at Versailles, there were many – especially French – who wanted to take an even harder line. When it came to the occupation of the Rhineland, Marshal Foch, commander in chief of the Allied forces, had argued forcibly that the proposed 15 years was not long enough. 'The Rhine alone is important. Nothing else matters.' He wanted the Rhineland occupied for at least 30 years, while reparations were paid and until the Germans had proved their good faith.[8] He warned the New York Times: 'The next time, remember, the Germans will make no mistake. They will break through into northern France and seize the Channel ports as a base of operations against England'.[9]

The terms of the treaty would be blamed for the rise of Hitler and the Second World War, but their impact was immediate and general. According to Richard J. Evans, Germany failed to make the transition from wartime back to peacetime after 1918.

> Instead it remained on a continued war footing; at war with itself, and at war with the rest of the world, as the shock of the Treaty of Versailles united virtually every part of the political spectrum in a grim determination to overthrow its central provisions, restore the lost territories, end the payment of reparations and re-establish Germany as the dominant power in Central Europe once more.[10]

At the time, the Press in the Allied countries presented different views of the treaty. On 8 May, the Daily Chronicle's headline referred to 'Germany's Day of Reckoning for her Crimes', while the Evening Standard reported 'German Anger At The Terms' and carried a warning from the New York Tribune that 'Not Since Carthage Has Such a Treaty Been Written'.

When the Germans returned to the Hall of Mirrors to sign the treaty on 28 June, the News of the World proclaimed: 'The Hun goes down in his wrath at Versailles'. One American newspaper, Frank Leslie's Weekly, headlined its photograph of the event as 'The Greatest Moment in History'. In such a context, it is not surprising that a little-known English-language newspaper published in Germany should have been so proud of its 'world's record scoop' the month before, 'a scoop that will stand to our credit for ever and a day'.

2. 'A British Newspaper For The Britons In Rhineland'

The Cologne Post's own story

The Post came about because everyone wanted it, thrived because of the dedication of all involved, and was a fearless friend to the entire community around the British occupation of Cologne.

That, at least, is how the newspaper presented its own history, when looking back in the final and farewell edition of 1929 on the eve of Britain's withdrawal from the Rhineland.

The Post's own vision of itself might be an accurate one, but some caution and context is needed. Newspapers, unlike some other historical artefacts, try to tell their own stories and often convincingly, too, given that they are staffed with professional communicators. A newspaper's story about itself will inevitably focus on its relationship with its readers and the world around it, laying out something that scholars of the mass media call a 'represented' relationship. That is, a relationship that the newspaper thinks it has, or wishes it has, or would like to be seen to be having, with the world around it.

The account of the 'scoop' – as has been seen – was the most significant story the paper told about itself, to counter any suspicion that it was a tame lap-dog with its claim to have defied the authorities in order to bring the news to its readers. But how did such a newspaper come into existence and how should it be viewed?

The true nature of the Post's place in the world will become clearer as the evidence for it is presented and analysed in subsequent chapters of this book. But as a starting point, the paper's own account of its origins and purpose is outlined here. It was a daily paper published in English from March 1919 to March 1925 to serve the British colony – both military and civilian – in the occupied German Rhineland. It continued as a bi-weekly publication from March 1925 to November 1929.

In the final 1929 edition, from which much of the following material is drawn, the Post's columns explained how the newspaper was created in 1919 to fill an information vacuum.

> At that time a journey to or from England took two clear days, and the Rhine Forces were two days behind current affairs. So the fiat went forth. 'A British newspaper for the Britons in Rhineland; a daily newspaper, the first issue to be published on March 31st.' [11]

Acording to J. H. Haygarth, writing in the final edition, this fiat came forth from the Military Governor General Sir Charles Fergusson, whose idea the Post was. Regardless of who invented it, the final edition was proud that 'our wonderful Army produced a small band of experienced journalists who looked ahead and saw the unparalleled scope for such a publication'.

> The business side of the adventure troubled them little, the great appeal to them lay in that the newspaper would be an asset of great value to Great Britain, and a guide and a friend to the men, sharing their troubles and pleasures, and stimulating them to the full consciousness of their positions. [12]

Operations began with a staff of just four men based in one room, starting work at 7am on Sunday 30 March 1919. They 'handled the news messages, wrote the articles, sub edited the matter, read the proofs, made up the pages, and saw the forms to the Press'. They secured Reuters news from home, sent over the military wire, 'on very generous terms'. The Koenig & Bauer printing press at the premises of the Kölnische Volkszeitung worked its magic, and the staff went back to their billets for breakfast and baths before returning to start on edition number two, working some 43 hours with barely a break.

The original cover price was 20 Pfennig. Army units were encouraged to order and pay for copies in bulk. By January 1922, with the impact of German inflation, the cover price had risen to 2 marks. Two years later, it cost 100 milliard (100,000 million) marks – but could also be bought for just one British penny.

What the editorial team were working for was explained in an editorial in the first edition on 31 March 1919. 'Our aim, then, is to make those who are here and those who are yet to come, feel more at home.' The writer added that the newspapers from home were not only too late, but did nothing to inform these new Rhineland Britons about what was happening on their doorstep, to them, or to their comrades. It wasn't just news that they needed, but 'sports, amusements, acquisition of knowledge, what to see, where and when to see it, and what it will cost you, what is today's value of 'ein Mark'.[13]

'These,' said the Post, 'will be published daily,' alongside letters and answers to questions about anything 'except perhaps such things as, say, demobilization.' Readers were encouraged to write in, as long as the content of their letters did not transgress the King's Regulations. Testing the boundaries could be interesting: in 1929 the newspaper said it had once carried a letter from a soldier, directed to the Government itself, with a request that the Government's response be carried in the Post's pages.

The newspaper also acted as a kind of search engine, a common practice with the press until the age of the internet, offering to settle any mess disputes by writing to ask the editor, for example, when the Lusitania was torpedoed, or when Crippen was hanged.

All this, the newspaper hoped, served the 'the sole aim of the Cologne Post [which] is to prove to every reader that it is his paper.'

The only thing the Post could not do, it seemed, was to publish photographs, as the German printing technology with which they worked was not up to the job. The technical difficulties were, according to the 1929 souvenir editorial, immense. German production processes were antiquated and 'would have sent Fleet Street compositors or stone-hands off their heads'. None of the German printers knew any English (and by 1929 only one of them did). Local inflation was another headache, causing the cost of the Post's production to rise by 600 per cent during 1919. Communications were vulnerable, too, with German peasants reportedly cutting telegraph and telephone lines, although there was no explanation of why they were doing so.

The Post's leader writer A. G. Clarke wrote in 1929 of the changing function and mission of the paper over the years of occupation, from its early days when its role was, for the thousands of young men so far from home, 'to offer a healthy English mental environment for spending the most impressionable years of adolescence among the subtle temptations of an unwholesome German town.' That, along with helping to facilitate English sports and entertainment, and via the 'Bummeling'[14] columns to 'show the young soldier how to make use of such unprecedented opportunities for true education' in their host country. Clarke notes that with the replacement of the original Army of Occupation by the regular Army, and the routines of garrison life, the paper's educational role was diminished in favour of the simple purveying of news as 'we ceased to become a glorious adventure and settled down to a more jog-trot existence'.

But the Post's own conceptualization of what such a newspaper should be is remarkably consistent in broadly these terms, despite changes in the size of the garrison. It saw itself as servicing not just the initially large occupation force but increasingly a diaspora or extended family. This was a repeated theme in editorials such as that of 3 January 1929, in which the Cologne Post & Wiesbaden Times (as it was by then) celebrated the New Year by stating that 'there is not one station of the gallant British Army to which the CP & WT is unknown on mail days'.

The British Army, more so then than can be imagined now, was a permanent global force staffed by those for whom home was a series of garrison towns and foreign postings. The Rhineland family was, as the garrison diminished and its mission drew to a close, increasingly scattered. These readers were addressed as expatriates, who needed news from the Rhine where they had served and where friends still did. The relationship was warm, mutual and somewhat clubby, as the 1929 New Year editorial continued: 'We look confidently to the support of our readers, so loyally given in the past, and in return we will not fail to keep them informed of the cream of the world's news. We will also provide a complete service of all Rhineland news of interest and a special sporting service...'[15]

The paper also defended that family against attacks by those back home who could never understand the nuances of occupation. It hit back, for example, at a Daily Express article which alleged that British soldiers were routinely playing soccer with Germans, calling it 'a gross libel on the British Army of the Rhine'. A couple of private golf and tennis matches had taken place, it said, but nothing more. Later, the Daily Mirror made the same error, and was met with another editorial:

> The Mirror gossip writer must be blissfully unaware that the CP and WT recently issued a challenge to the Daily Express to prove its statements concerning Rhine Army teams meeting German teams ... he must also be unaware that several English newspapers referred to the resentment felt by members of the BAOR at this libel upon them.[16]

At the level of actual families within the Army family, the Post facilitated social life with, for example, the Children's Club, which was similar to those in popular newspapers back home though, in this case, children could join by writing in to 'Uncle Ebenezer' giving details of their name, age and father's rank and unit. There was also the In Woman's Realm page, 'conducted by Winifred', giving advice on, for example, how to wear the latest jewellery.

It seems that this idea of the Army family, and the Post as its friend, was not a fiction. Some years after the death of the first editor, Captain Rolston, the newspaper ran in its tenth anniversary edition (in 1929) the following piece. Headlined 'Mrs Rolston's Congratulations', it read: 'Just before going to press last night a telegram reached us from Mrs Amy Rolston, widow of Captain W. E. Rolston, our founder and first editor. The wire read, "Splendid tenfold congratulations and further good wishes".' The family was keeping in touch, through the good offices of its newspaper.

There were opportunities for the wider Army family to educate and improve itself by, for example, reading the long and often charming pieces on such subjects as Military Symbolism, written by the mysterious Athelstan Ridgway. Although frequently bylined, there was no hint of his authority to write such pieces beyond his way with words and what seemed a considerable and eclectic knowledge. Another of his pieces ruminated on the decline of the great house, and the need for a gong to summon people to dinner.

The tone of such pieces was rarely patronising, and never hectoring, instead maintaining the kind of stance one might expect from a wise but affectionate member of that family. When it came to politics, for example, a column bylined simply 'Periscope' dealt swiftly and fairly with the General Election of 1929 welcoming the revival of the Liberal Party, and writing that 'it seems to me that we want always to have a party that hits the mean between extremes of Conservative and Labour,' before carefully adding that 'all three parties have good points'.

The Post could, however, rise to the occasion in cases of ritual at the heart of occupation life. It devoted page after page to occasional reports on military ceremonials, such as the King's Birthday Parade, often in advance and providing an intensely detailed procedural manual for those taking part or observing. The tone and relative infrequency of these reports is akin to that of the present-day BBC's ability to switch from impartial to dutiful for the coverage of royal weddings and such like.

This returns us to the question of the Post's status – official, independent, or somewhere between? A newspaper's financial underpinning is often a way to examine that in terms of who holds the purse strings, but even in that the Post is somewhat opaque, at least from a century's distance. The very idea of taking advertising, for example, (at least for German businesses) raised some eyebrows, with a question being asked in the Commons in 1919. The Post rebuffed the criticism, asking how else soldiers could know of goods and services of which to avail themselves.

How else, too, could the newspaper defend itself against another claim, that of ill-using public funds, without trying to raise its own? There had been, the Post reported, protests from unspecified quarters regarding the use of public money to finance a 'private venture'. But senior officers in the Rhineland spoke up for the paper whenever they could, and according to its own description in the 1929 edition it was in fact '... a semi-official organ. Its columns often contained much that was intended to convey an official point of view to the German readers. Not that it was propagandist in any invidious sense, but, rather, that it was informative on the true aspect of big political issues'.

It was indeed a curious newspaper, receiving some support from the state or the military establishment, yet making its own money; toeing the establishment line, yet also apparently free to carefully invent its own.

Ridgway, that mysterious and verbose feature writer, emerged from the shadows in the final edition to reveal more about this semi-official status. He writes that there had been speculation in Fleet Street about his own role, and although he had presented himself as a kind of uncle or 'deus ex machina' (his phrases both), pulling a few strings here and there, he was also a co-director of information at the War Office.

Ridgway mentions that the Post had some initial help from the Army Council but when it made £1,000 in profit, was asked to pay it back. It eventually did so, with five per cent per annum interest, but only after 1923 when the paper's finances grew stronger under the managing editorship of J. H. Haygarth. It was then that it changed the strapline on its masthead from 'A Daily Paper published by the Army of the Rhine' to 'The Oldest Established British Daily in Germany'. And this would explain the change in status indicated by two statements to Parliament about the paper. In 1919, the Secretary of State for War (Winston Churchill) told MPs the paper was 'under the control of the General Officer Commanding the Army of the Rhine'[17]; in 1925, his successor stated that the War Office could accept no liability for the action of the paper's management, as it was 'not financed from Army funds, and is not an official publication'.[18]

There were further instances of official assistance for the Post, according to Ridgway. To help the newspaper get timely news from beyond the Rhineland, for example, he arranged for the daily telegraphing of up to 800 words of Reuters news from room 423 at the War Office. However, with another nod to the Post's financial and thus perhaps other forms of independence, it was charged £500 per year for the service. The Post was not selling enough advertising to pay that bill so a compromise was reached, with a reduced wire service offered, padded out with Foreign Office and other official dispatches. Friends on Fleet Street chipped in with tidbits and the Aldershot Command Signals took over the wiring. So, it seems, the price of the paper's free service was to receive (and presumably publish) a little more official news; its financial plight gave the authorities that leverage.

Ridgway describes how advertising took off, with almost half of one 14-page edition being devoted to it, but acknowledges that the Germans who placed adverts (looking for work as governesses and so on) did not always pay up. The Post's team was able, perhaps due to some financial success, to launch a four-page Oppeln edition when most of the garrison was stationed in Upper Silesia in 1921. But by 1925 the newspaper was hit by what it describes as its darkest days thanks to the crashing of the Mark. Captain Haygarth (the BAOR's Amusements Officer) was asked by the General Staff to take it over as managing editor, thanks to his expertise in matters financial. This suggests again the hybrid status of the Post – subject to arm's length oversight by the military command, but with the desire for it to have some financial independence. The latter tends to be accompanied by editorial independence – the BBC, for example, maintains its own relatively hands-off relationship with the state via the subtle workings of the licence fee.

By the time of the Post's closure, it was painting a picture of that editorial independence, a picture of the newspaper as having bravely triumphed against adversaries from within - as well as outside - the British establishment. In a by-lined piece, with an accompanying photograph of himself in civilian dress, A. G. Clarke reveals that he has been the leader writer for most of the past eight years. 'We have ever striven to keep any party colour from what we have written,' he writes. But he is passionate about the battles the Post chose to fight on behalf of its readers. 'Time after time this paper has been "killed" – "killed" [he must have meant nearly killed] by a wildly fluctuating Mark, "killed" by the axes of would-be economists ... "killed" by distant officials who knew little of its influence.' We know not who the distant officials were; only that they did not prevail.

What was the Cologne Post? It is tempting to seek the sinister in its story – some sense that this was a faux-friendly newspaper covertly funded by the state for the purposes of propaganda of even the most benign kind. Certainly the careers of some of its staff, attached to the Intelligence Corps, and the trajectory of at least one of them later, could contribute to such speculation. One of its leading journalists, Harry Maule-Ffinch, did after all go on to work on BBC programmes transmitted to Europe in English during the Second World War. These included The Man in the Street broadcasts, and the talks to Europe's Underground Movement by (the fictitious) Colonel Britton. Maule-Ffinch, a Post veteran, thus went on to operate in an environment in which a news organisation otherwise jealous of its independence from the state became its servant, producing propaganda during a national emergency.

That grey area between journalism and propaganda was, anyway, never so grey in the era of two world wars or even after. Maule-Ffinch and his peers were doing journalism at a time when newspaper proprietors such as Beaverbrook and Northcliffe made no secret of - at the very least - tub-thumping on behalf of Britain and Empire. Northcliffe's Daily Mail, for example, had campaigned for naval expansion and war with such vigour before 1914 that when the war finally came his seaside home in Kent was shelled by a German ship, in what may not have been an accident. Both men, despite being the barons of a free press, felt able during the Great War to serve, one as Minister for Information (Beaverbrook) trying to rally the allies and the other as Director of Propaganda (Northcliffe) targeting the enemy. The collusion between journalists and the state may, therefore, have seemed even more natural between and during two total wars, and sensitivities about it not hard to handle for the Maule-Ffinch generation of journalists and broadcasters.

But the Cologne Post, in contrast, was never so obviously engaged in propaganda or pushing a state message, aside from recognising its duties to report without restraint on military ceremonials.

To interpret its status one need not look at a stark choice between voice of the Army, and the voice of the soldier. It was instead a curious hybrid, seed-funded and partly aided by the state at a long arm's length, yet financially independent enough to deflect the charge of it being a burden, and all the time wise enough to draw its own editorial boundaries rather than wait for them to be drawn. To occupy such a grey area, over such an extended period, was a considerable achievement in itself. Chapter 9 explores ways in which the paper developed an editorial policy which can be compared to that of the BBC, which emerged - like the Cologne Post - in the changed social landscape of the post-war world.

3. Journalists In Uniform

The men who made the paper

The story of a newspaper can be told many ways, whether in terms of paper, printing, politics, machines, and machinations, but in the end it's a human story and in the case of the Cologne Post a particularly vivid one.

It starts with a mass of humanity gathering as the Great War ends. After the armistice of 11 November 1918, those remaining of the five million Britons who wore military uniform began to be scattered. Some were demobilized – steadily, for fear that the arrival home of so many fighting men without jobs, but with a hard-earned sense of entitlement, would be vulnerable to the revolutionary fervour sweeping Europe, collapsing empires and dynasties in its path.

Others remained in service, to police the new uncertainties: some as part of the short-lived intervention force in the post-revolution Russian Civil War, on the collapsed Eastern Front, hoping to both prevent Germany securing a foothold there and to halt the spread of Bolshevism. Others were involved in the Irish war of Independence from 1919-1921; or served in further-flung corners of the Empire to take part in, for example, the Third Afghan War.[19]

Another contingent, often overlooked in histories of

the period, began moving from the Western Front towards the frontier of Germany itself. They were ready to police the post-war settlement being worked out by the allies and which would involve the occupation of, at least, Germany's Rhineland. By early December the mission for some of them became clear: already on the outskirts of Cologne, British forces were to cross the Hohenzollern Bridge and set up what was to be the headquarters of their zone of occupied Rhineland, where they would stay until 1929.

> The cavalry went in on 12 December 1918, and according to General Sir Herbert Plumer '...at 10 o'clock the Union Jack was unfurled and the troops commenced to cross. The band of the Blues played them past, men and horses looked splendid'.[20]

Within the ranks on the move were men from all walks of life; some scarred by war, others able to take the opportunities arising from it. And although many of the more minor players in the Post's story remain in obscurity, amongst them were those who would take leading roles in this curious episode of journalistic history, and sometimes beyond, each of them in their own way a product of their times.

We do not know whether or not he marched across that bridge to the sound of the band, but we do know that the leading figure in the story of the newspaper that would serve the British Army of the Rhine (as it was known by March 1919) was Captain William Rolston.

He was a Cambridge astronomer, son of a Birmingham thermometer-maker, and attached to the Intelligence Corps by the time he reached Cologne. Living with the lingering effects of wartime gas duty, he became founder editor of the Post, and worked himself to death, leaving behind in his billet three cameras and a typewriter – and a widow in London.

Then there was Captain Harry Maule-Ffinch, son of a district surveyor in Malaya, and a journalist on the Malay Mail before the Great War, which he joined as a member of the Artists' Rifles. He survived the war and the occupation (although it appears his brother died on the Somme) to serve next time around – but as a journalist with a leading role in the BBC's psychological warfare against Nazi-occupied Europe.

Some of what we know of these men and their comrades on the Post is detailed in the pages of the newspaper itself, especially in anniversary features, some from records held at the National Archives in Kew and some in obituaries.[21]

Something is known of Rolston's early life. He was born in Birmingham in 1876 and it's his birth certificate that lists his father's occupation as a maker of thermometers. The technological tendency seemed to rub off on young William, and was nurtured in Birmingham at the George Dixon School, which had been founded by the city's eponymous campaigning MP as the Bridge Street Technical School in 1884 and specialised in the teaching of science and mechanics.

From there Rolston went to the Royal College of Science in London, and then to Cambridge University, during which time his own description of his occupation changed from school master to astronomer. He was a notable figure at the university's Solar Physics Laboratory.

It was at Cambridge that he acquired the military experience, via the Officer Training Corps, that would encourage him to apply for a commission in May 1915. He wrote to the Commanding Officer of the Royal East Kent Regiment, or the 'Buffs', that he had heard from the Master of Jesus College that there were vacancies for officers and thought the Buffs might appreciate his experience in the teaching of map reading and compass skills to cadets.

By the next year, he had developed the health problem that may have plagued him during his latter service on the Post. He was believed to have contracted an infection, manifesting itself as a lip ulcer, from the wearing of an infected gas mask in 1916. The problem is recorded in the report of a medical board in London in February 1917, which noted that he had twice been tested for the disease. The source of infection mattered, because army medical forms noted whether any disability was acquired through circumstances outside the soldier or officer's control. If your own recklessness had made you ill, then you might be punished for it through 'hospital stoppages' which meant no pay during the treatment period. Rolston was not in that category, for his sickness was ruled to be the direct result of his service.

His ailment was noted again in a report of 1917, but this time there were no external symptoms, and he was cleared fit for service subject to treatment and the passing of a blood test at a military hospital.

Rolston was fit enough to spend the entirety of 1918 in France and Belgium, with the Fifth Battalion, The East Kent (Territorial Force), attached to the Intelligence Corps. As the war ended he arrive in the occupied Rhineland, and by 1920 was given a clean bill of health at age 43, with no reference on the medical report to his previous troubles or any others.

According to the Post's final and farewell edition of 3 November 1929, the newspaper's founders alongside Rolston were Captain E. Ingham, Lieutenant E.T. Moore, and Sergeant Major Nevill. The last was an experienced journalist, who worked as the editor's assistant, before eye trouble laid him low. After his recovery, he worked as a Reuters correspondent in Western Germany. Captain J. H. Haygarth, writing in the final edition, relates a long list of names of cashiers, clerical workers and the rest, and mentions Herr Charles Opitz, the compositors' foreman, who had 30 years experience in England.

But the more significant players for whom some traces remain included Colonel Cranston,[22] Haygarth himself at the helm from 1923 (combining the role of managing editor with that of Amusements Officer to the BAOR), and W. Le Crerar, who deputized frequently for the editor, and even went to London to report on football for the Post.

As the pioneering team established the Post's reputation the newspaper reported it had gone on to recruit: 'Professor Main of St Andrews University, now a well known figure at Balmoral, Sapper J.W. Ogilvie, an Aberdeen journalist'. Then 'Lance Corporal Jimmy Griffiths, of a Liverpool paper, Sergeant J.P. Quinslisk, a Yorkshire journalist, Captain Ferguson, of The Scotsman, the late Lieutenant Baker, who left us for The Times...'

Others included a Corporal P.J. Finnigan who went on to write for a Catholic newspaper; London journalist Lieutenant C.P. Sisley; Lieutenant Jimmy Dunn who went on to work with Thomsons; Lieutenant R.H. Gibbs, an Oxfordshire journalist, and 'Harry' Maule-Ffinch who it was reported had by 1929 gone to work for the Bristol Times and Mirror.

The precise trajectory of later careers remains obscure in many cases, but Rolston's own story is a tragedy and well-documented. He was found dead at his billet in Cologne on 9 August 1921, aged just 45. The report by medical examiner Major Blashford of the Royal Army Medical Corps in the BAOR, noted that:

> The body was that of a very under-nourished man ... cause of death was embolism followed by cerebral haemorrhage due to an unsuspected cardiac condition and most probably arising during active service while serving as Gas Officer in France.
>
> This officer had been strenuously and continuously occupied in sedentary work in an office, and unable to take exercise or obtain relaxation ... death in my opinion was ... exaggerated by the continuously exacting work which accelerated and in all probability led to his death.

According to another document, Rolston left behind in his billet in Maria Ablass Platz, three cameras, one Oliver typewriter, one lens, one pair of field glasses, a battery, and various clothes. In addition he left a widow, who had just set out from England to visit him in Cologne, and was intercepted in time, thanks to swift action by the Army, which is detailed in a series of poignant telegrams in the archives.

Rolston's death deprived not just his family, and journalism, but above all science, as is clear from the obituaries. Who knows whether this polymath would have dedicated the next two decades of his working life to the army, journalism, or astronomy. His remains are in the Sudfriedhof cemetery in Cologne.

In another case, however, a great deal more is known of how the media career of one of the Post's staff was intertwined with military service, journalism, and propaganda.

Knightley 'Harry' O'Dowd Maule-Ffinch was a son of the Empire, born in Kandy, Ceylon, in 1896, which happens to the same year of birth as the Daily Mail, that prototype of popular mass market journalism that would set the scene for a century of middle market newspapers.

He worked as a journalist with the Malay Mail, during which time he reported on the Singapore Mutiny of 1915, but also served from June 1915 to March 1917 in the Malay States Volunteer Rifles, as a territorial. He acquired some knowledge of Malay and Tamil, which marked him out later on the papers that processed him into the regular army and a commission. The officer filling in that form did not tick the boxes for skills in musketry, bombing, anti-gas, machine guns, riding, or technical. Indeed, he made a note that Maule-Ffinch was not able to ride, but added that he 'should do well, after some experience'. That experience began with a move to London as a private in the Artists' Rifles, which had been formed in 1859 in response to fears of French invasion, and was filled with artists, musicians, writers and other creative types. Along with other London volunteer battalions the Artists' fed into the London Regiment, with which Maule-Ffinch served as a lieutenant in France and Belgium from August 1918.

Although he survived apparently unharmed, being given a clean bill of health in a medical report of August 1920, it appears that his brother Eric Maule-Ffinch fell at the Somme. The brothers had earlier been mentioned, as a pair, in a letter of 28 February 1918 from the 2nd Artists' Rifles Officer Training Corps, recommending them both for service in the London Regiment. Four years later, a woman who appears to be their mother was writing from an address in Paddington, London, to the military authorities enquiring about a pension or compensation regarding her son 'E.H.J. Maule-Ffinch [who was] killed in action in the battle of the Somme, August 27 1918'. Her husband, she said, was without work, and without income she was in dire straits; had her son survived he would, she was sure, have provided for her.

By March 1919 it seems that the surviving Maule-

Ffinch brother was with the Army of Occupation in the Rhineland and, by August 1920, according to his medical report, was being described as of the 7/London regiment, 12 KRR (Kings Royal Rifle) Corps, attached Cologne Post.

After Cologne, Maule-Ffinch found himself back on civvy street and continued in journalism, of a sort, with the Radio Who's Who[23] providing a handy record of what sort it was. After 'many press posts abroad,' it says, he returned to England, and in 1929 became night Editor of the British United Press News Agency, which supplied overseas news to the BBC.[24]

When the Second World War broke out Maule-Ffinch joined the BBC Overseas News Division, becoming English Editor – that is, in charge of news and programmes transmitted to Europe in English. He was made a Member of the British Empire (MBE) in the 1956 New Year Honours.

Last but not least is the mysterious Athelstan Ridgway, who wrote long and improving features for the Post but rarely revealed the basis of his authority. That is, until the newspaper's closing days, when he described himself as not just a kindly 'uncle; supporting the paper's efforts but also co-director of Information at the War Office.[25]

That, then, is what remains of the stories of the men who crafted the Cologne Post, with Maule-Ffinch's and Ridgway's careers and roles hinting at the complex status of this unique newspaper.

4. What's In Today's Paper?

A close look at the Post's content

The Cologne Post can be found today in the archives at the British Library in London. Dust falls from between well-preserved pages that appear to have been unopened for a century. The newspaper has been digitized[26], but the researcher who handles the hard copies is perhaps more able to recreate some of what its readers would have experienced upon picking up their local newspaper.

What follows is a 'walk through' of the paper on two occasions, each some years apart to capture the changing nature of the garrison and the journalism that served it.

The mode of analysis is inspired by that of the journalism history scholars Barnhurst and Nerone[27], who write of the way readers 'swim' through a newspaper – and suggest that researchers do the same in order to capture a qualitative and holistic impression of all that contributes to a newspaper's identity. That includes dimensions, headlines, number of stories, lengths of stories, categorization and signposting, use of imagery, bylining and sourcing.

The editions selected for analysis are typical daily (and later bi-weekly) Posts, rather than those skewed for example by major scoops or the intense coverage of set-piece events such as military parades. There is some comparison of the two editions, but the aim is more to put the reader in the place of the reader back then and by doing so elicit some points about what the Post was trying to be, and what it really might have been, for those readers.

The first edition in question is Thursday 1 January 1920, chosen because of its sheer ordinariness (nothing in the coverage suggests that the day was anything but a normal working one). A soldier picking up this edition would have been greeted with a newspaper measuring 60cms high by 40cms wide, thus about the size of four A4 sheets of paper in total, with a front page loaded with some 40 stories arranged neatly across six columns. It was unrelieved by any imagery (including display advertising, for page one contained no advertising) and the editors refer in other editions to their disappointment in technical problems preventing them from reproducing photographs until much later in the 1920s.

The reader is nevertheless helped in his navigation of the page somewhat by headlines stacked in decks of two or three lines, depending on the weight of the story beneath. The content was not especially related to the Rhineland.

The main story of the day was the inquest into the Phoenix Park murders in Dublin and the rest were fact-heavy news reports from Britain and the world with an emphasis on the Empire and post-war Europe. Only one story appeared to be of specifically local interest: a summary court report regarding a Rhineland German who had stolen a bottle of whisky from a Briton.

The Post had across its pages a total of 126 discrete editorial items (excluding advertising) to read. The Post's editors offered something of a guide to the reader, after the avalanche of news on page one, with the signposting of sections on the inside pages.

There, our reader would have found much of page two dedicated to meandering editorials about the success or not the of the peace settlement, alongside others on the future of the British pub, mixed in with anecdotes about military life such as the misery of amateur garrison music. To the right, the page carried a column headlined 'The Editor's Letter Box' with seven pieces of correspondence from Rhineland soldiers regarding such matters as the price of whisky in the mess, the poor quality of amusements, some congratulations on the prowess of the Post's artist, and a poem.

On the facing page, three, was sport across four columns: inter-allied running, a BAOR soccer cup tie replay, national sport reports and results including horses at Cheltenham, and more. Then came two columns labelled 'Amusements and Recreation', mostly Rhineland in nature and including reports of two garrison-related weddings, details of the Cologne Opera House programme, and the football coupon. Our reader's final page, four, contained at its centre a striking two column drawing with the satirical caption 'An Easy Guide to German Official Dress', showing six different functionaries from postman to porter and all points in between all dressed identically. The 'Echoes from The Rhineland' section had local news snippets of a paragraph each; the foot of the page had a miscellany of home news and anecdote called 'Notes from London Town'. The right hand column headlined 'From Everywhere' contained 31 crisply-written paragraphs of news from, indeed, everywhere, each about 20 words long and with its own two or three word headline.

When it comes to advertising, any newspaper may find the quantity, and indeed sometimes its ratio to editorial space, varying according the health of the economy. But for this edition the front page carried only news and no advertising (there were, later, rare occasions where the entire front page was given over to advertising). The advertising appears on page two, where it takes up two and half columns, thus amounting to about eight per cent of the area of the pages in total. Even some of that, however, was 'house' advertising with the Post promoting itself and thus earning no revenue from that space. For example, the paper used a display advertisement to wish its readers a Happy New Year, with a line drawing of an attractive young woman in a fashionable hat and the slogan 'She enjoys the Cologne Post. Make a New Year Resolution and send it to her daily.' The rest of the advertisements are for tailors; Kodak printing; the Inimitable Illusionist Mr Hugh Herring appearing at the YMCA in Cologne; the Aladdin pantomime at the Metropole nearby, various concerts; the sale of Spanish wine; and the announcement of the engagement of Frank Hedgcock of the NACB RASC to Berthe, youngest daughter of Eva Bornstein of Warsaw. There seemed to be no reluctance to take advertising from German businesses.

The Post's journalists are not visible on its pages. There are no by-lines on the news stories, and only vague ones at the foot of letters and comment pieces, often in the form of nicknames. This was mostly in keeping with widespread British journalistic practice at the time, with the lack of personalisation shoring up the coherent, authoritative, voice of the newspaper itself rather than of the individuals who produced it. Indeed, for a small staff possibly multi-tasking as well as depending heavily on agency copy, it had the additional benefit of suggesting a monolithic operation rather than the scrabbling around of a few overworked reporter-editors. Certainly, the Post was not in the habit of flagging up very often the provenance of its news by attributing agency copy, or even stories lifted from day-old British newspapers, where it seems likely to have been so.

By the later 1920s the garrison had diminished, the First World War was as far away as the next one, and the occupied Rhineland had become a settled posting capable of supporting family life. Newspapers from home reached the garrison faster, and there was radio to listen to. The Post itself had ceased daily publication and become a bi-weekly.

A soldier – or indeed by that time a member of his family, or other civilian – picking up a copy of the bi-weekly Cologne Post and Wiesbaden Times (as it had become since the British move from Cologne) on Thursday 28 January 1928 would have found the newspaper changed, too. It was a much smaller, tabloid size. The pagination had risen to eight and the appearance of the front page was neater, more organised, using a three column layout and with only 14 stories on it. The mix of stories remained global and local, with the newspaper leading on a British ship going down in the North Atlantic, and adding stories such as a murder trial from Worcester, and some sport (tennis from South Africa and racing from Newbury). Rhineland news came and went on the front page, but on this edition it carried four paragraphs on the visit by a senior allied officer, and (rather oddly) a continuation from the page four 'Echoes of the Rhineland' column, containing four BAOR stories such as the opening of a school for officers' children, sales at the shops, and church service times.

Inside, page two was remarkably consistent with the same page in our previously sampled edition: a leader on international affairs, and some lightweight, humorous, discursive columns including comment on a man-eating tiger in India. Much the same occupied columns on page three, this time under the heading 'Our London Letter', bylined 'Periscope' (and written by Athelstan Ridgway), offering lengthy wit on such matters as literature, fashion, and the funny ways of Americans. The right hand column contained what one might call news you can use – an update on how soldiers could pursue emigration to Australia.

Page four was made up mostly of the 'Echoes' column combining a piece on interesting places to see in Wiesbaden with some procedural detail about garrison organisation, then an entire column of British soccer results from home. The fifth page was for British racing tips, local church service details; page six for football pools and advertisements; page seven for a serialised fiction ('The Conquering Flame – Dick and Joan on the brink of a precipice'), and page eight was devoted entirely to advertising.

Gone, by 1928, were the long columns of local BAOR sporting fixtures and results, and some of the sense of adventure of the early days of occupation. The newspaper might have looked rather more like an expatriate newspaper for a small number of guests in someone else's country. There was far more advertising, amounting to nearly six columns out of 24, thus around 25 per cent of the newspaper. Much of the advertising was from German businesses appearing to have a settled relationship with a garrison now ten years old. This was a newspaper adapting to its mission, in some sense showing signs of decline by the 'padding' of lengthy and inconsequential ramblings in the place of harder news which was either not happening (in the case of the diminished BAOR presence) or was being reported adequately elsewhere (in the case or British and global news).

Even up to the end, however, there seems little evidence that the Post was anything but a professionally run newspaper that could - in terms of craft skills when it came to reporting, writing, accuracy, headlines, tone, design and production - hold its own against a Fleet Street or British regional equivalent of the day. But it is as important to identify what was missing from the Post, in comparison with its counterparts back home. It seldom thundered (apart from when its readers were slighted), it was not partisan, and it did not propagandise or otherwise seek to convince its readers to believe this or that. The only exceptions were its suspension of a critical approach on the occasion of military ceremonies, when it seemed obliged and/or content to clear the decks for intense detail about such things as where one should stand and what one should do and for how long.

In terms of what else the Post did not do, we might add the addressing of its readers, even subtly, as consumers towards whom it pushed a lifestyle in league with the advertisers. There appeared no need for it to act with such commercial drive, beyond simply making ends meet. One might assume (though we cannot confirm) that the soldier-journalists' salaries were paid by the Army, and that any surplus revenue was used to pay for operational costs such as wire copy, paper, compositor wages, printing and distribution. Profits and riches, for the staff or publisher or shareholders, are nowhere mentioned and neither is the pursuit of them apparent.

That is not to say that the Cologne Post was bland. One might find some clues as to what the newspaper meant to its readers in the very fabric of its construction, as outlined in this chapter. It was made, as seems very clear, as the readers' own newspaper: a mirror to their world so they might know it better; a leader when required, yet sometimes leading on behalf of the Army itself; a forum for discussion within the constraints of military discipline; and a marketplace for goods and services that the community might find useful. Above all, there was a sense of the Post as a collaborative venture between its publishers and readers, with the former facilitating rather than trying to influence the lives of the latter.

BRITISH SUMMARY COURT.

POSSESSION OF REVOLVER AND KNUCKLE DUSTER.

Hans von Borkenhagen, of no fixed abode, was brought up in custody charged with being in unlawful possession of arms, i.e. a revolver and knuckle duster. He pleaded "Guilty".

A German policeman related how he found the weapon in a trunk in accused's lodgings when he had occasion to make a visit there in connection with another charge. The weapon is a revolver of a cheap type, but serviceable. No revolver ammunition was found, however.

The accused said that he was an architectural student. He had only in occupied territory some fourteen days and he did not know the regulations. He had purchased the weapon from a fellow apprentice, and intended taking it with him to America when he goes soon. He said that he had had the knuckle-duster for a good number of years.

5. 'Germany Should Be Taught Her Lesson'

How the Post reported on relations with the occupied population

Adolf Hitler stood before a court in Munich on 26 February 1924, accused of high treason during the 'Beer Hall Putsch' on 9 November the previous year. It was the moment when he first came to widespread public attention in Germany and beyond – and a moment he used to put down a marker for the future. The trial was the lead story in the Cologne Post next day.

> This afternoon Hitler spoke for four hours, his main theme being a strong defence of the Nationalist movement. He delivered a vigorous attack on the Berlin Government, whom he repeatedly described as the 'November traitors' ... He said during the course of his impassioned speech, which was delivered with much gesture, that he believed in a Germany extending far beyond her present boundaries. (27 February 1924)

Hitler's first move to restore Germany's boundaries came in 1936, when he sent troops into the demilitarised Rhineland in defiance of the Versailles and Locarno treaties. As he spoke in court, Allied troops still occupied the Rhineland and, for more than a year, French forces had been in control of the Ruhr, where they would remain until July 1925.

While Hitler was haranguing the Munich tribunal, a British officer, sitting as President of the Summary Court in Cologne, heard the case against one Wilhelm Hover, accused of overcharging a British soldier for a 'second class' bath at the Kaiser Wilhelm Baths in the city. The Post reported that he was fined 200 billion marks.

The size of the fine was indicative of the level which Germany's hyper-inflation had reached by the time Hitler and his National Socialist Party launched their Putsch. As Richard J. Evans writes: 'The process of monetary depreciation was taking on a life of its own. The political consequences were catastrophic'.[28] A billion marks was one million million.[29]

German civil courts continued to operate in Cologne during the occupation, but German citizens could be brought before the Summary Court for offences 'in the nature of breaches of orders issued by the British military authorities, acts to the prejudice of the British Armies, or offences against the persons or property of British or Allied subjects.'[30] Once the Peace Treaty had been signed, breaches of the ordinances of the Inter-Allied Rhineland High Commission (IARHC) would be tried before the summary courts.

During the first few months of the occupation, up to 40 cases a day were heard in the summary courts in Cologne. Respectable citizens 'who had never thought that they would be involved in criminal proceedings, learnt in this way what the inside of Klingelputz Jail looked like'.[31]

As late as 1921, a highly respectable German citizen was brought before the Summary Court. Julius Nacken was accused of 'breaking through the ranks' of British troops on the march. He explained that he was hurrying to work – as a judge at the City Court. The Post reported an unusual encounter:

> Presiding Officer: 'I have never had a fellow judge in front of me before. I suppose I ought to punish you severely as a fellow judge, but I do not think you will do it again. Discharged.' Whereupon Judge Nacken made a deep bow and retired. (4 June 1921)

The reports of the Summary Court cases in the Cologne Post shine a light on relations between the occupiers and the occupied at the points where the relationship was most strained. And the juxtaposition of these accounts alongside reports of political events in the rest of Germany gives a unique perspective on the occupied territory and the troubled country to the east.

The Post reported the verdicts in the Munich trial on 2 April 1924, under the headline 'Mild Sentences for High Treason'. Hitler's accomplice General Erich Ludendorff was reportedly 'ashamed' to be acquitted. Hitler was sentenced to five years imprisonment in a fortress and a fine of 200 gold marks – but could be released after six months and 'bound over' to be of good behaviour for the remainder of the period. The paper's correspondent wrote:

The sentences, to say the least, are ridiculously mild. One German newspaper, commenting on them, remarks that they are a travesty of justice. (2 April 1924)

On the day Hitler was sentenced, it was a case of 'Street Bolshevism' which occupied the Summary Court in Cologne. In the adjoining column on the front page, the Post reported a case involving an attack on a British officer's car – an offence against the dignity of His Brittanic Majesty's Army. The defendant was jailed for three months - half the time Hitler would serve.

> The accused had pleaded that he lost his temper, but the President [British military judge] did not accept that excuse. Persons who admitted failure to control themselves must be controlled. People in Cologne always failed to realise that the roads are made for vehicles and the footpaths for persons walking. 'There is too much of this Bolshevism about in these days.' (ibid.)

Self-control and respect for the dignity of the Occupying Army were part of what the British had to teach the population of the occupied Rhineland. As the Post put it in an early leader column, under the heading 'Citizen Soldiers':

> We are really a British colony of British citizens who are showing a defeated enemy the ideals which inspired us in the war and which are still untarnished. (1 August 1919)

There is an echo here of arguments advanced by earlier supporters of Britain's imperial 'mission', convinced that the British had evolved to be a nation uniquely suited to teach the lessons of 'ordered liberty' to others. Benjamin Disraeli said it was not the Navy or the Army which had created and maintained the empire, but 'the character of the people'.

> Imperialists believed that the early development of a system of ordered liberty was the reason for England and Britain's commercial and industrial success, and had allowed it to expand into the world via trade, migration, religion and language, all of it underpinned by growing naval and military strength. ... It also encouraged the notion that the British nation had a predestined, perhaps providential, role to play in global evolution.[32]

The British courts were not as lenient as the German tribunal which sentenced Hitler and his co-conspirators. The Munich sentence contrasts with that meted out later in 1924 to a young German nationalist accused of membership of the Stahlhelm Bund (Steel Helmet Association), an organisation associated with the Freikorps of ex-German soldiers, who formed a standing armed force over and above the officially-limited army of the Republic. Wilhelm Gerhards 'a young man of smart appearance and distinguished bearing' was jailed for three years by a special British military court for membership of a paramilitary organisation forbidden under the ordinances of the Inter-Allied Rhineland High Commission.

Evidence was given of a raid by a British officer accompanied by German police on a Cologne café, where 10 to 15 men were found sitting around tables on which were statues of Bismarck and the former Kaiser, a black and red flag, and a steel helmet. The Cologne Political Officer of the Commission produced the orders banning the Stahlhelm. The court also heard that the organisation within the occupied territory had been disguised under a false name, but that the founding documents proved its purpose of resisting reparations, fighting the 'war guilt lie' and restoring to Germany all territory lost as a result of the war: 'Every comrade is honour bound ... to act up to its principles even if it means death'. The Post quoted the defendant:

> 'I only want to say that what I am doing is purely from patriotic motives, and if England were occupied by us as this area is by you, you would probably do likewise.' (17 September 1924)

The territory which the British Army took over in December 1918 covered almost the whole of the Department of Cologne (Regierungsbezirk Köln) with 1,250,000 inhabitants. Of these, 600,000 lived in the city, 'the metropolis of the Rhineland, the seat of the Government of a Department, a fortress, a great manufacturing city, and one of the most important railway centres in Germany.'[33]

Looking back in 1926, after the Army had left Cologne for Wiesbaden, the Post put a positive gloss on the first contact between the occupiers and the defeated Germans. Praising their 'dignity and self-control' (no 'street Bolshevism'), it claimed that 'the great majority of the respectable people and law-abiding citizens' were relieved at the arrival of the British, whose mounted troops moved through the streets 'without fuss or arrogance'.

> When our cavalry patrols entered Cologne and rode to the Hohenzollern Bridge in the early days of December 1918, so being the first British troops to reach the Rhine, they did so at the express request of the Bürgermeister[34], who was afraid of anarchy. The retreat of the German Army had been marked by looting and mob violence and the red flag of revolution had been raised. The municipal buildings had been 'captured' and the mob had proclaimed itself in possession of civic authority. .... In those far-off days the Germans behaved with dignity and self-control. Whatever their feelings in that hour of bitter trial ... they were hidden under a mask. (24 December 1926)

Things did not continue as smoothly as the Post's account of the first contact. David G. Williamson describes a clash of cultures which probably explains the number of cases appearing before the Summary Courts in the early months.

> Two different worlds clashed: a large military pres-

ence with its own organizations and way of life was superimposed upon the civilian population. Consequently there was friction at almost every level between soldier and civilian.[35]

Until the Peace Treaty was signed, the Army of Occupation remained at full strength and ready to resume the war by advancing into unoccupied Germany from the bridgehead established on the left bank of the Rhine (the eastern part of Cologne). In the first months, relations between German citizens and the British were tightly regulated. Fraternisation was banned and German men were ordered to salute British officers by removing their hats. But the Post – in hindsight – saw the treatment of the Germans in a positive light:

> Very quickly it was brought home to them that the orders and regulations which were issued were not marked by any spirit of revenge. Our Occupation was not harsh, though strict, and while it was but natural that the towns-people should resent the inevitable restrictions, they openly acknowledged the fairness, justice and courtesy of the administrative officers. (24 December 1926)

As early as May 1919, the paper had reported complaints in the German press about the terms of the occupation, but it compared them favourably with the regime imposed on Belgian and French cities like Lille by occupying German forces during the war. Later that year, as the strength of the occupying force was drastically cut following the Peace Treaty, the Post painted an idyllic picture in a leader column, which gave 'Tommy on the Rhine' the credit for 'a complete absence of resentment at our presence'.

> It is no idle boast to say that the Tommy as a class has endeared himself to his hosts. His unassuming, easygoing nature and high sporting qualities have made their appeal, until strange as it may seem we have the spectacle of men, women and children deploring the impending departure of the greater part of the British Army of the Rhine. 'Better twenty years of British rule than one of Bolshevism' said a Rhinelander in the early days of the occupation. ... The most inimical Teuton is not slow to realise that since the occupation he has enjoyed far greater freedom and less exercise of officialdom than before the war. (11 September 1919)

However benign the British (and the Post) believed their occupation to be, resentment endured. When the remains of the occupying army withdrew from Cologne to Wiesbaden in January 1926, the Oberbürgermeister Konrad Adenauer celebrated 'the hour so fervently longed-for':

> The day of freedom has dawned. ... We have had seven long years to bear a heavy burden under the hard fist of the victor. ... We have borne suffering in common.'[36]

In his memoir of four years of the occupation, R. G.

Coulson (writing as 'Apex') suggests that many of Cologne's citizens had not had such a hard time under the victor's fist:

> Among the population, especially among the women, there must have been many who found it difficult to realise that they had been such heroes.[37]

As the Post's Letter Box shows (see chapter 7) there were heated debates about what relationships were acceptable between the British and the Germans (especially German women). The paper had made its position on fraternisation clear in one of its first leader columns, recalling Germany's breach of Belgian neutrality, the sinking of the Lusitania, 'vile' submarine warfare, and the treatment of prisoners:

> It is inconceivable that any Englishman should make friends with people who have committed such ignominious outrages during the past four years. ... At all times let us be courteous to the enemy, but never let it be said that we, who have been honoured in the privilege of forming part of the Rhine Army have defiled the memory of those who sacrificed their lives in order that Germany should be taught her lesson. (3 April 1919)

Two months later, men of the 3rd Light Trench Mortar Battery debated 'at great length and with considerable force' on the question of whether fraternisation should be permitted. The Post reported (15 June 1919) that the 'anti-fraternizers' won by an almost unanimous vote, following which 'a sing-song rent the (otherwise) peaceful night air'. Who needs to fraternise when you can make your own fun?

As the older, battle-worn troops were replaced by young soldiers who had not seen the horrors of trench warfare, the paper was moved to warn them against an overly open display of 'that friendliness which the man in the ranks cannot help leaving behind him as part of his sunny nature wherever he goes'.

> We know the temptations in and out of billets, to fraternize. Kindness, perhaps is not forced, but in the background is that inheritance handed on by the men whose bones are rotting on the battlefields of France and Belgium and by whose effort, in part, our presence on the Rhine was made possible. The young soldier should keep this before him and he will not then go astray. (29 June 1919)

In spite of concerns about fraternisation, the Cologne Post, from the first week of publication, carried advertisements from German businesses in the city keen to attract the attention of almost 300,000 potential customers. These dealings with the former enemy stirred up controversy at home and on 1 May 1919, Hansard reported that the matter had been raised in the House of Commons by Horatio Bottomley MP, who had been a leading propagandist for the war effort. He asked Winston Churchill, Secretary of State for War, whether his attention has been called to advertisements of German firms appearing in the 'Cologne Gazette' (sic) which is described as a daily paper published by the Army of the Rhine; whether the Army authorities have any control over such paper; and, if so, whether directions will be given for the exclusion of such advertisements in future?[38]

Churchill replied that the Cologne Post was under the control of the General Officer Commanding the Army of the Rhine and that he had asked for a report on the matter.[39]

It may be no coincidence that a month later the paper carried a notice directing any potential German advertisers to its special agent and stating that 'all advertisements are subject to the editor's approval'. In a feature on its first anniversary, the Post reflected on the ups and downs of the previous year – including controversy over its advertising policy:

> The few German advertisement which did appear in the first and later numbers brought us a storm of abuse. Articles were written denouncing this 'preference' to our then enemies and questions were asked in the House of Commons. In reply we propounded a simple question which quashed the argument. If a British soldier in Cologne wished to be shaved or to drink a glass of wine, must he wait until his turn for leave came round in order to avoid patronising a German?' Anyhow, we stuck to our original principle, while Peace was yet afar off, by accepting only such

advertisements as did not clash with British interests. (31 March 1920)

The paper went on to argue that it was the only medium by which German manufacturers could bring their produce to the attention of British merchants or consumers and claimed that its advertising columns had acted 'as advance agents to many transactions of enormous magnitude.'

The development of trading relations between British and Germans went alongside continued political friction. As the paper celebrated its second anniversary, it reported the latest news about a 'Communist Rising' in the unoccupied Rhineland. Alongside that account was a report that a Cologne newspaper had been suspended by the German civil authorities in the city for a related offence against the ordinances of the IARHC. Under the headline 'Inflammatory Articles in Socialist Organ', it stated:

> The Communist outbreak in Central Germany appears to have inspired the wildest and most irresponsible of statements, many exhortations to take an active part in the Communistic 'fight'. ... Such practices can only tend to lower the prestige of the German press. (31 March 1921)

Interestingly, in that same edition, an account appeared by a special correspondent for the Morning Post under the heading 'Briton and German in Cologne', concluding that the occupation was 'less popular than formerly' – especially because of the ordinances of the IARHC, which Germans complained was 'more autocratic than the Russian Tsar ever was'.

> The British interpret these Ordinances as liberally as prudence permits, and leave the maintenance of law and order primarily in the hands of the German authorities, but the very fact that the Ordinances are in force and that they are, in effect, laws is naturally galling to the intelligent German. The municipal authorities contend that the situation is unendurable, and that it is impossible that the Rhineland Commission shall continue to exercise supreme authority regardless of local opinion or feeling and shall continue to try German civilians before courtsmartial. Many civilians coming before the British military courts were accused of minor offences such as overcharging members of the occupying army, stealing property from barracks or billets, or possession of weapons prohibited under the rules of the occupation. (31 March 1921)

In one such case, the intervention of a British officer was not enough to protect a respectable German citizen from the impartial justice of the Summary Court. Under the headline 'Rich Man's Rusty Revolver', the Post reported that a partner in one of Cologne's largest firms had been charged with unlawful possession of two revolvers and a bayonet. He told the court they were souvenirs and a British Major testified that he had known the accused for over 12 months, describing him as 'a most respectable man'. The weapons were rusty and of no use, he said.

> Presiding officer: 'I cannot convict a poor man for having arms in his possession and a rich man go scot free. If he had reported them to the police it would have been alright. 500 marks or 21 days – but on his security that he does not intend to make any other use of them he may hang them up on his wall for decorations'. (27 March 1920)

R. G. Coulson ('Apex') records the indignation felt by some of those who fell foul of the regulations and the courts. In 1924, through family connections in Cologne, he was invited to dinner at a country house outside the city. There he met Baron Shimpworth, who had been fined that morning in the British military court for illegal possession of arms.

> The military police had come into his house, he said, walked straight up to some attic and pulled out a sporting rifle which he had not used since the beginning of the War, and had quite forgotten about. Someone must have denounced him to the military police: a discontented servant girl with a soldier friend, probably. He had been put in the dock like any thief, with no consideration for his rank. The Court had taken no excuses and had fined him forty marks.

The baron went on to complain about the treatment of Germany, the French occupation of the Ruhr and their deployment of black colonial troops. He accused the

British of hypocrisy in their attitude to France's policy.

> 'I tell you today, five years after the War, we see what peace is like. We see how you have met our efforts at reconciliation; and we prefer open war to this peace.' He banged the table so hard that the plates jumped, and several glasses upset. 'If we want revenge today, then you and your Allies have driven us to it.'[40]

Coulson reported that in his own time with the special branch of the military police his main job had been investigating complaints against Germans - many of them 'quite futile' - from British officers and officers' wives, 'who obviously suffered from an over-developed sense of their own dignity'.

In one such case, the Post reported (11 June 1920) that a German landlord and his wife had been summoned after complaints from a British officer billeted in their property. They were accused of failing to comply with an order to supply hot water in the bathroom daily, removing two armchairs and 'insolent and threatening behaviour' when the officer ordered the return of the chairs to his lodging.

When British wives were billeted in German homes along with their husbands, there was even more scope for friction, according to Dr Josef Beckers:

> Even in her kitchen the German Hausfrau was no longer the boss. She had to share it with the wife of a British officer, NCO or private soldier, who was often full of pride and arrogance at the defeat of Germany

> ... The shared use of the kitchen all too easily caused dissension, quarrels and even assault.[41]

During the period of hyperinflation, Cologne was described as 'the Island of the Blest' for the British, whose purchasing power was greatly increased by the depreciation of the German currency. For the Germans, it was a very different story. Coulson described a case in which 'an apparently decent man' was arrested for trying to procure his daughter as a prostitute for a British soldier. She had refused to co-operate, but the Special Branch of the Military Police concluded that 'conditions in Cologne being what they were, the girl had been wrong to refuse; the family needed the food so urgently that to keep her personal chastity was a mere luxury'. Her father was not brought before the court.[42]

The British authorities repeatedly emphasised their political neutrality, and despite his complaints about the 'hard fist of the victor', Konrad Adenauer acknowledged that, politically, the British had always been 'scrupulously fair'.[43] But if political activity breached the ordinances of the IARHC, the courts took action.

In May 1921 Germany had been plunged into the first great crisis over payment of reparations and a threatened French occupation of the Ruhr district. That month, a newspaper editor was jailed at the summary court (10 May 1921). It was alleged that he had breached the ordinances by calling for a general strike to bring down the German government. His defence appealed to the British notion of free speech, but the Presiding Officer sentenced him to three months in prison, pointing out that, in 'the peculiar circumstances' of occupied Germany, 'conditions could not be the same as those in England.'

Troops from the French occupied zone advanced into the Ruhr in January 1923 to enforce German payment of reparations. On the day this was reported by the Post, it carried a front-page account of a case in the summary court at Solingen (outside Cologne) against a town councillor who was Chairman of the Communist Party in the district, accused of holding a political meeting without giving the 48 hours notice required under IARHC ordinances. The presiding officer made his position clear:

> As I have often said in this court, the British Authorities take no interest in politics whatsoever and I do not wish to prevent the holding of political meetings – it is not my business – but an order has been made that 48 hours notice of intention to hold a political meeting must be given. (11 January 1923)

One consequence of the occupation of the Rhineland was the growth of support for an independent Rhineland Republic – an idea which, it was often alleged, was supported by France and Belgium, in the interests of establishing a permanent and sympathetic buffer state between them and Germany. The issue came to a head – just weeks before the Munich Putsch - with the declaration of a Rhineland Republic at Aachen (in the Belgian-occupied area) on 21 October 1923. There were demonstrations and buildings occupied in the French occupied zone at Trier, Koblenz and Mainz. Two days later the Post

– crediting wireless from London – reported that shots had been fired in Mainz. Police in Aachen had been firing 'from behind women and children', while there were reports of a Communist rising in Hamburg.

Next day, the summary court heard another political case involving the organiser of a paramilitary nationalist group called the Jung Deutscher Orden (Young German Order), accused of holding a political meeting in the British-occupied zone, without giving the required notice. The defendant claimed it was simply a social occasion at which beer had been drunk. The presiding officer again emphasised that the British 'had no desire to interfere with political feeling, nor to prohibit meetings', but the rules were the rules.

A more serious case was that against a German Communist who was tried by British court martial in May 1924 on charges of counterfeiting, unlawful possession of arms and participating illegally in military training. He was alleged to have been in possession of engraved plates for counterfeiting German one billion mark notes and British pound notes.

> The accused, Jacob Frantzen, a leading member of the Communist Party, appeared in court in a shabby suit, limping badly on one foot, his thick black crop of hair cut in the approved Communist style. (22 July 1924)

The Post reported that he was convicted of all charges and would be sentenced once the Commander-in-Chief had considered the case.

Another Communist fell foul of the British three

months later (13 September 1924), for publishing an article – based, it was said, on a forged document – alleging that the British authorities and the German police in Cologne were conspiring against the interests of one political party. The editor of the Sozialistische Republik, 'the official organ of the Communist Party for Rhineland and Westphalia', was charged with publishing a document prejudicial to the safety of the Armies of Occupation and publishing a newspaper likely to prejudice public order or endanger the security and dignity of the High commission and troops of Occupation. The first prosecution witness was the Political Officer of the IARHC, who said he received copies of all the papers published daily in Cologne. The editor was cleared of endangering the safety of the Army, but jailed for six weeks for publishing false evidence, which the presiding officer ruled did indeed prejudice the dignity of the High Commission.

The dignity of 'His Brittanic Majesty's Army' was a touchstone of the British sense of their mission in Germany. It extended to the wives of soldiers and there were several cases before the summary court in which Germans were accused of behaving without the necessary respect towards British women. In one case (11 June 1920), two young German women were alleged to have insulted the Swiss-born wife of a British lance-corporal. Hearing her speak German to her sister, they had shouted: 'She is not English. She is a city whore!'

His Brittanic Majesty's Armed Forces were prepared to insist on proper behaviour when necessary. In a case which epitomises the sense of how the British saw themselves and their role in occupied Germany, a town mayor was made to apologise in public 'for the insult offered to Capt. G. Lawson M.C. the Representative of Inter-Allied Rhineland High Commission in that area'. The officer, 'wearing H.B.M.'s uniform' and travelling in an IARHC car went to the town of Wald on duty during Communist disturbances on 29 March 1921. He was subjected to insulting remarks 'by a crowd of irresponsible people', some of whom attempted to overturn the car. 'The attitude of the Town Authorities was reflected in the inactivity of the local German police and no effective measures were taken to cope with the dangerous attitude of assumed by the mob.'

To atone for the insult, the Mayor and the full town council were made to stand in front of the Town Hall while a detachment of infantry, Lewis Gunners, and 'a very well turned out troop of Military Mounted Police' (MMP) presented arms to the IARHC Commissioner for Cologne and a colonel representing the British Army of the Rhine.

The town councillors were described as 'a curious looking lot of people ... as little like the British equivalent as could be imagined'. Having removed their hats, the Mayor 'was ordered to submit the apology, which he read out in a clear voice'. The Post published the full text in German and English. The Mayor concluded:

> 'Such events can only disturb the good co-operation of the British governors and the German people in this district. The town of Wald, through me, expresses hereby to the British Occupying Authorities, the High Rhineland Commission and the representatives of the

Imperial British Uniform its request for pardon.' (8 April 1921)

Accepting the apology, the Commissioner warned that such occurrences could, under no circumstances, be tolerated in the British Zone.

After the reply, Mr. Piggott inspected the M.M.P. and then drove off through a large crowd of inhabitants, amongst whom were hundreds of children who may remember, with advantage, the historic proceedings of the day. (ibid.)

Some of those children may have recalled that experience when, 24 years later, they witnessed the return of His Brittanic Majesty's Army to the Rhineland as part of a renewed effort to 'teach the Germans a lesson'.

6. Home On The Rhine

The British colony seen through the pages of the paper

'The Rhine Army not only has its own dress, language, business and family life, schools, hospitals, clergy, amusements and sports, but even its own newspaper ...'[44]

During the course of 1919, the British community on the Rhine experienced a series of changes, beginning with the early demobilisation of the rank and file who had fought the war and their replacement with young soldiers who had been conscripted before the armistice but had not completed their training. Many of the wartime officers and NCOs remained in Cologne.

In his account of the occupation, Ferdinand Tuohy, a journalist who served with the Intelligence Corps on the Rhine, describes the next big change as the decision to allow officers to bring their wives to Germany.

> Indubitably that which most altered and coloured life in Cologne was the arrival of the wives under an order of Sir W. Robertson's. When these were allowed

out to join their husbands, bringing with them a first batch of sixty children ... their presence worked a social revolution. Billets from bricks and mortar, became homes. And the B.A.O.R. began to tingle ... and to assume that self-contained, almost segregated air which was to characterize it for the remainder of its life.[45]

Within ten days of the Cologne Post's first publication it had printed a letter suggesting that officers should be able to bring their wives to Germany. It was after German acceptance of the Peace Treaty that women were permitted to join their husbands. In August, the Post reported that a hotel in the city had been taken over and converted into quarters for married officers. The amenities were compared 'to those that can be enjoyed in the comfortable quiet family hotels in the West End of London'. By September, it had begun publishing a regular feature 'for the British Woman in Rhineland', which was only one of several innovations designed to maximise readership among English-speakers in occupied Germany and beyond.

In March 1920 Freikorps troops taking part in the Kapp Putsch against the German government wore swastika symbols on their helmets and painted them on the side of their vehicles.[46] This was one of the first recorded uses of the historic 'Aryan' device associated with the forerunners of Hitler's National Socialist Party. Only a few months earlier, the wives of British officers could have read, in the Cologne Post, a recommendation of the symbol as a fashion item:

> The curious little harbinger of good luck, the swastika, embroidered on a light mesh ground is quite a popular design. (5 November 1919)

The paper's new Vanity Fair column appears to have been syndicated and made no specific references to Germany, Cologne or the life of the its female readers. The content was largely focused on fashion – led by London and Paris. The first feature predicted that 'the fate of the very short skirt is sealed'. On the same page, as a regular accompaniment to the column, was an advertisement for 'Venns Undies'. (As early as 25 July, the paper had carried its first advertisement targeting women readers – a half page promoting ladies' coats from a London fashion house.)

There is plenty of evidence from the pages of the paper that the arrival of women in the garrison ruffled the feathers of some of the 'old school' of soldiers who had become accustomed to solely male company during the years of the war. One such correspondent greeted the arrival of Vanity Fair with an ill grace, regretting 'the good old Army days, when man ruled supreme'. Another, 'heartily sick of the sight of khaki' welcomed the arrival of women in the dining rooms, but drew the line at their 'invasion' of the reading room of the Navy & Army Canteen Board club.

Publication of a feature for women readers seems to have driven some of the 'old school' to pen misogynistic pieces for the paper, which the editor was happy to publish. One 'spoof' on military regulations outlined the rules for 'Transport of Wives' in cases where they had to travel unaccompanied from Britain. They should be carefully labelled and 'where necessary, gagged'. Powder puffs should be carried 'as these are unobtainable on the ships'. Another 'regulation', headed 'Behaviour', ruled: 'The practice of calling Husbands in public "Dinkums Doodlums" is on the increase. This practice must cease forthwith.' (23 November 1919) The previous day a cartoon had depicted a woman at a mirror under the headline 'Fares, please!'. 'Now that British ladies have to pay for their joy rides on the Cologne trams, Mrs Me Brassat practices how to say "Funfundzwanzig" and look sweet at the same time.'

This sequence of jibes and complaints provoked a heartfelt response from one British woman, concerned – among other things – about the impact such language could have on impressionable young male members of the British community in Cologne. The Post headlined it 'Chivalry on the Rhine'.

> Are the men who criticise so very different from the men we served in canteens, or nursed in hospital? War strain – yes but women had it too; that awful waiting has left its mark. It has become habit to hide real feelings under a laugh, but do not let us forget that the laugh may probe someone else's wound. Here in the Rhineland, where many a young soldier is forming his ideas, it seems a dangerous place in which to lower the ideal of womanhood. (21 Dec 1919)

Misogynistic complaints had been printed before the arrival of the officers' wives. Members of the Women's Royal Air Force were accused of 'chatting, giggling and eating buns' during a performance at the Opera House. Correspondents moaned that 'the girls at home' had developed undesirable habits and failed to appreciate the charms of Tommy home on leave. There were also letters questioning the impact of wives' presence on officers' military efficiency. The debate even reached the pages of the Daily Mail in Britain, prompting the Post to print a leading article under the heading 'the Wife on the Rhine'.

> For years the British Army has provided for the living together of husbands and wives ... If in Rhineland, as is alleged, a husband here and there, owing to the propinquity of his spouse and the attractions of the Perfume City, is not performing his duties satisfactorily, there are official ways and means by which the delinquent can readily and easily be chastised, and obliged to reform his erring ways. (24 Sept 1919)

The YMCA opened the first hostel for wives of 'Other Ranks' in November 1919 and the Post reported that premises were being sought to provide more, in spite of the scarcity of accommodation in Cologne at the time. The wives of British soldiers were officially part of the Occupying Army and entitled to the same respect as men in uniform. Several cases were reported in the paper in which Germans were prosecuted in the Summary Court for insulting British women. To make their status clear, they were expected to wear a distinctive armband or 'brassard', though it appears many forgot or chose not to do so. At one period in 1920, the Post's letterbox was overwhelmed with correspondence on the subject. When the editor published the last letter on the subject, he declared that 'this correspondence must now cease'.

> Why should there be so much objection to wearing them? We have already heard the objection as to the blouse not suiting the colour etc., but when a lady goes out for a walk she generally has a jacket or similar garment on and I have not yet seen one on which the colours would clash. Now then, every British lady visiting Rhineland, do not be ashamed of your nationality but wear your armlets and show everyone that you are British. (10 June 1920)

In July 1919, a correspondent had asked 'Why only the married?' He argued that unmarried 'English' girls should be allowed to come to Cologne - 'how else will Tommy find a wife?' In fact, though discouraged by the Army, hundreds of soldiers found wives outside the British community, among the German population. By September 1921, 150 'other ranks' and seven officers had married Germans and by 1925 the number had risen to 700. The German wife of a British soldier became an official member of the occupation forces and exempt from most German regulations.[47]

Looking back on ten years of occupation in its final edition in 1929, the Post recalled the changes in the British community which followed the arrival of the Army wives.

> The introduction of British ladies into our midst created a new social system. British family parties were to be found in the Opera House, the fine restaurants and in the Military theatres, of which we had three in Cologne. The ladies joined their husbands in amateur theatricals, several of them acted with the British Rhine Army Dramatic company, which was then a professional company. River steamers were chartered and every Sunday these steamers plied their way up the Rhine to the beauty spots between Bonn and Bingen, usually drifting back to Cologne, in the moonlight, between 10 p.m. and midnight. (3 Nov 1929)

The post-war period was a time when women were challenging male dominance – a fact which the Post's writers welcomed, up to a point. While it was not until 1928 that all women got the vote, the first female MP to take her seat in the House of Commons was elected in November 1919. Lady Astor's campaign prompted comment in the paper. Under the heading 'Women in Public Government', the writer welcomed the prospect of their 'essentially conservative' influence in a troubled time:

> I believe it to be of enormous value that the women's voice and will should come into actual power at this time when there is so much unrest, so much reckless expenditure, so large a proportion of revolutionary

thought. For woman is essentially conservative. In spite of much that has been seen of late in the way of careless spending, of exaggerated pleasure seeking, of 'emancipation' carried to extremes, these things are true but of a small proportion of our womankind, and are probably even with them but a temporary symptom of War conditions and later reaction from the strain. (19 November 1919)

A syndicated feature by Annie Swan, published the following year (21 July 1920), commented that male politicians were right to be afraid of the women's vote. 'It is going to count tremendously, and it will without doubt give an entirely new complexion to public affairs.'

'Agnes', the writer of Vanity Fair, warned against 'the post-war spirit of restlessness and adventure which is so strong and prevalent among women workers of all sorts at the present'. They should find their job in life 'and stick to it'.

It is one thing for a woman to be a pioneer and to have the courage of her convictions; but a woman who is constantly jumping from one sort of work to another like a cat on hot bricks injures the mass of women workers. (16 Sept 1919)

While Vanity Fair focused almost entirely on fashion and housekeeping, there were occasional items – either in the column or beside it – which showed a broader interest in women's lives and place in society. One suggested that women were showing themselves better at public speaking than men, 'now they have the chance'.

> The average woman speaker is crisp, succinct, and often witty. She marshals her facts, makes her points, and leaves you wishing that she had spoken for a longer time. All this is well, for with woman entering public life by every door, and in some cases having to overcome prejudice, it would be unfortunate if she added to the evidence against her the crime of boring those obliged to listen to her views and her interpretation of her own position. (21 July 1920)

One area in which women in Cologne made their views clear, according to Ferdinand Tuohy, was in the attitude of Army wives to the German population and the hot topic of fraternisation. He believed their hard line contributed to the isolation of the British community in Cologne.

> It is on record that some of these British women hardly saw eye to eye with their menfolk in regard to a certain 'poor old Jerry'. They did not like the gentleman, even in the beaten and cowed edition, and they said so.[48]

Other observers described social contacts 'on the upper levels' as non-existent.

> Many of the English families now living in Cologne can hardly be conscious that they are in a foreign country. The English military community lives a life apart. At

hardly any point, except in the shops, do they come into contact with the Germans. The large majority of English people, men and women alike, do not speak the language, and few make any effort to learn it.[49]

The Germans were regarded in much the same light as the natives in any other foreign station: to mix with them would have occurred to no-one.[50]

By early 1921 there were around 1,600 Army families in and around Cologne, adding 5,000 Britons to the military population of 10,000. By 1922, there were an additional 2,500 British civilians or 'Colognials', many of them ex-officers or soldiers who chose to stay on the Rhine after demobilisation rather than face unemployment at home. There were also German immigrants, who had been interned in Britain during the war, who were forcibly repatriated and chose to settle in Cologne because they were 'in essence more British than German'.[51]

This community was supported by the complete range of British institutions which Percival Phillips had noted (quoted at the head of this chapter). The Post was credited with inspiring the establishment of the first school for the children of servicemen. Lady Robertson, wife of the BAOR's commanding officer, formally opened it in November 1919. Dr Francis of the YMCA, a regular contributor to the paper, said a letter to the editor had led them to establish what was in effect a comprehensive school before its time. It then had 42 pupils.

The school is held at the Central Y.M.C.A. and there is no distinction of sex or class. Boys and girls work together and knight's son and squire's son receive the same instruction. (25 Nov 1919)

This classless society was not for everyone. In 1922, the paper carried an advertisement for a boarding school for 'the sons of British gentlemen' at Mehlem, south of Bonn. The principal was Capt. H. W. Noakes, former headmaster of naval cadet training ships 'assisted by a qualified staff of university graduates'. The following year the Post advertised a school 'for Officers' Children', which highlighted the offer of 'rhythmic dancing classes'. On the same day, the paper promoted - 'For the Kiddies' - its own book room stock of 'English picture books at English prices'.

Outside school there were Scout and Guide troops. In 1923, the Post reported comments from the Scoutmaster, Capt. Gibson, about the challenge of scouting on the Rhine, singling out 'a lack of helpful home influence' and warning that 'the many grown-up attractions taken in too large quantities are very bad as far as boys are concerned'. In 1924, more than 200 Guides and Scouts were on parade to welcome the Chief Scout and Lady Baden-Powell, in the presence of the Commander in Chief of the Rhine Army. After watching a display of lifesaving from a 'burning' building, Lord Baden-Powell told the children they were doing more than becoming good citizens – they were part of the mission of the British Watch on the Rhine.

You are an example to the people in the midst of which you live, and I hope that your example will be followed by them, so that these boys and girls who watch you here on the Rhine may become good citizens too. (1 April 1924)

After the 1925 relaunch of the paper as a smaller, bi-weekly publication, a regular feature for children was carried under the title of the Cologne Post Children's Club, written by 'Uncle Ebenezer'[52] who was introduced as 'a gentleman who has had extensive experience of writing for a well-known home paper'. There were competitions for different age groups and puzzles: 'Q. Why is a Britisher like nineteen shillings and elevenpence? A. Because he is under a sovereign' (unlike the occupied Germans who had lost theirs).[53]

Vanity Fair had been discontinued in 1923, but was replaced in the bi-weekly paper (in May 1925) by a feature called In Woman's Realm 'conducted' by 'Winifred', who was said to have enjoyed a long experience as 'Lady Editress' of a well known home weekly. The content was similar to that of its predecessor, with an emphasis on fashion and housekeeping. One of its memorable tips was a new use for an old cricket bat, which 'may be converted into a splendid sleeve board for ironing'.

By 1925, British wives on the Rhine may have been doing their own ironing. In earlier years, they would almost certainly have had a servant to do it for them. During the hyperinflation which brought misery to the

Germans, the British colony on the Rhine lived like lords and ladies. Cologne, in the early 1920s, was known as the 'Isle of the Blest'.

> About this time the mark, which at the beginning of the occupation was 20 to the £, began to fall heavily and the troops with their valuable sterling, became men of great power and wealth, eagerly sort (sic) after by the natives. Everything was absurdly cheap if bought at the right moment; a good overcoat could be bought for 3/-, champagne from 2d to 6d a bottle and many people bought German boots at less than 1/- a pair. Higher and higher was the mark inflated and one morning, in twenty minutes, it had dropped (or risen) from 16 billions to 56 billions to £1. The British community took full advantage of these conditions, travel tours were indulged in, Cabarets, Theatres and Chars-a-banc did record business. It was at this time that Cologne was recorded as the most prosperous place in Germany, thanks, of course, to the British money that was spent there. (3 Nov. 1929)

The life of the British community would change drastically once the German economy recovered, making life on the Rhine a very different experience. Social amenities which had been provided for the British for free or at a nominal cost, were closed.

> In the autumn of 1924 what a change came over the scene. The recovery of the mark from 60 milliarden

to 16 marks to the £ in one day, immediately turned the wealthy Britisher into an impecunious person, and the natives, for the time being, took over the reins of millionaires. A German worker's wage, previously equivalent to 10/- per week, became £10 per week, consequently the troops and their families had to find their luxuries and entertainments in their own circle. (ibid)

For the remainder of the occupation, those who had known the early years did indeed look back on them as a blessed time, when the British community in Germany enjoyed a lifestyle very different from those around them – and from many of their compatriots at home.

The Editor's Letter Box.

MORE OPERA TROUBLES

TO THE EDITOR OF *THE COLOGNE POST*.

Sir, — It was very pleasing to note in this morning's issue a letter and also in your first issue, a small paragraph dealing with the question of behaviour at the Opera House.

That such remarks should appear so early in your paper seems to me a testimony of your future value. At the same time I must regret that such letters have need to be published, especially in a country crammed full of people straining their necks to find out our weaknesses and comment upon them. The Major who wrote your yesterday letter dealt fairly fully with the grievances of opera lovers. But one important point he omitted, and that is smoking. People go to the opera, I presume, because they like to hear, and they like to hear the very best that can be given. Yet one cannot expect an actor or an actress to give of his or her best in a room beclouded with smoke. It is grossly unjust and inconsiderate to those who have to use their voices for such a lengthy period. Then again, to smoke in a close room with little ventilation is to undermine one's own health and comfort. It may seem quite paltry, but nevertheless it is true and serious.

I hope your paper may be the means of making an alteration in the seemingly paltry yet highly-important features which at present mar all the beauties and benefit of opera-going. —

FADDIST.

7. The Editor's Letterbox

How the readers of the Post 'fashioned a knowledge of themselves'

In her study of letters to the editor, and journalists' relationship with their audience, Wahl-Jorgensen (quoting Jürgen Habermas) describes the letters section as 'one of the few places where "society as a whole fashions a knowledge of itself" – a place where members of diverse groups can gather for a shared conversation about the issues that concern them all.'[54]

Historically, it has been seen as 'among the few outlets available to the public for voicing opinion', 'a debating society that never adjourns'.[55] The letters columns of the Cologne Post can clearly be seen to fulfil this function, in a new community which was feeling its way to a sense of identity in the transition from war to peace in occupied Germany.

The Editor's Letterbox was just one of the ways in which the paper explored and articulated this sense of community. Its editorial – or leader – columns were another focus for this exploration, sometimes responding to issues raised in correspondence from readers. And its news priorities, the emphasis it gave to particular stories, also reflected the paper's view of the values of the

English-speaking readers of this 'British newspaper for the Britons in Rhineland'.[56]

In a very real sense, the British in the Rhineland – as seen by the Cologne Post – were, in Benedict Anderson's phrase, 'an imagined community'.[57] The 'Watch on the Rhine' was underpinned by a set of shared values, apparently understood and occasionally articulated. In an early leader column, under the heading 'Citizen Soldiers', the Post expressed its conception of a readership with which it closely identified:

> We are really a British colony of British citizens who are showing a defeated enemy the ideals which inspired us in the war and which are still untarnished. (1 August 1919)

This spirit can be identified in the prominence the paper gave to its report of a visit by Lord Baden-Powell to inspect Scouts and Guides on the Rhine in 1924. The Chief Scout told the children they were doing more than becoming good citizens – they too were part of the mission of the British Watch on the Rhine.

> 'You are an example to the people in the midst of which you live, and I hope that your example will be followed by them, so that these boys and girls who watch you here on the Rhine may become good citizens too.' (1 April 1924)

A poster advertising the paper in the days before its first issue stated that the editor would 'be pleased to hear from you at any time on any subject, Army or otherwise'. Other early statements in print emphasised the idea that the Post belonged to its readers:

> If the paper fails to publish what you want to know, write and demand an answer; for it is your paper, and its duty is to give you what you want – except perhaps such things as, say, demobilization.

When it came to correspondence:

> In our 'Letter Box' column we are always quite ready, within the limits of our space to insert any comment, any 'grouse', any opinion, so long as it is understood that we take no responsibility for it, or that it does not blatantly transgress the soldier's multilogue, K. R. [King's Regulations].

The Letter Box itself often carried a sub-heading: 'Our Readers' Varied Views' or 'Our Readers' Varied Views on Many Topics'. The 'ears' alongside the masthead on the front page encouraged readers to send in their opinions or complaints: 'Got a grouse? Write to the "Letter Box" about it' or simply 'Write to the Editor's Letter Box about it'.

> 'We hear all sides and accept no responsibility for our readers' views'. (Sub-heading on The Editor's Letter Box, 7 October 1919)

On the face of it, the Cologne Post encouraged correspondence and ruled out only discussion which might clash with military regulations (in an army which was, in the early months, still on a war footing). But it cannot be assumed that the range of topics covered in the published letters represents the make-up of the post-bag as a whole. There is no way of knowing what proportion of letters received were printed, nor what was the content of those the editor chose not to publish. What criteria did he apply in making his selection – and how did the statement that this was 'your paper' influence him in assessing 'your' letter?

While many studies take it for granted that the letters section constitutes a 'public forum', it is editors who are the gate-keepers, deciding – as Wahl-Jorgensen puts it – 'not merely who is allowed to speak, but how and why they may speak'.

> They ... construct the public debate by picking which letters they publish. As one editor put it, 'I like to look at it as a marketplace of ideas, and part of my job as an editor is to decide what's a reasonable idea'.[58]

It is not known whether the Cologne Post was a profitable venture, but there is ample evidence in its pages that it was run on a commercial basis. Advertising revenue was clearly important, but it also employed a number of strategies to engage with its readers and increase circulation – among the military and the wider potential readership of an English language newspaper in Germany. The Letter Box may have played a part in this. The paper certainly promoted it and early on, boxes were placed in the officers' clubs to make it easier for readers to send their contributions.

Wahl-Jorgensen interviewed a range of later newspaper editors for her research. She quotes one who emphasised the value of letters in building a readership – a small marketing tool, but one that works. Another expressed the importance of letters in this way:

> 'Letters to the editor help foster a sense of community. A newspaper is a business, and we have to make a profit as a community newspaper. We can only do that if it feels like we're helping out the community.'[59]

In its 10th anniversary issue, in 1929 the paper recalled the impact of the Letter Box:

> The Post ran a Correspondence Column in its youthful days, and it is interesting to record here that one soldier wrote to a great Department of State requesting that an answer be given to a query he put forward, through the columns of the Cologne Post, as the subject was of interest to the whole Army of Occupation. The Department complied with his request and courteously asked the Cologne Post to give the answer publicity. We did. (31 March 1929)

The paper published readers' letters regularly for its first two years, but not after 1921. The number of troops in the British Army of the Rhine fell dramatically from the original occupying army of 273,000. In 1920, it was 40,000; in 1921, 12,000; between 1922 and 1925, around 8,000. The decline must have had a great impact on the paper's circulation and may have accounted for a drop in correspondence.

In the early days, the Cologne Post served a very clearly defined community, which included men who had shared an experience of war and killing on a scale never known before. The memory was powerfully invoked in a letter taking issue with a judge in Britain, who had referred to a man in a divorce case as a 'common soldier'.

> Does Mr Justice Horridge know, that it was men whom he stigmatises as 'common' soldiers who saved him from the same fate as hundreds of French and Belgian civilians. Men who perished for England at Mons, the Marne, the Somme, Ypres, deserve a better name than this. (8 July 1919)

There was a two-way interaction between the paper and its correspondents. Sometimes they responded to what they had read in the Post; at other times, the paper followed up its readers' concerns. In what may have been a response to receipt of the above letter, the leader column addressed the issue on the same day.

> In no manner of means can the wearer of khaki be regarded as 'common'. Rather is he an individual whose standing should be a passport to the best which our social fabric has to offer. (Leader, 8 July 1919)

Correspondence was published on a wide range of subjects, some topical, some of particular interest to the army, some whimsical or obscure. The earliest letters, published just months after the horrors of the fighting in France and Belgium had ended, focussed on what should be the shared values of the British on the Rhine in what now seems a surprising context – behaviour (or misbehaviour) at the opera.

> I refer to the behaviour of our troops, particularly the officers, at the Cologne Opera House .... a large number seem to have very little idea of how to behave in such a place. (1 April 1919)

Perhaps surprisingly, letters about the opera and the conduct of the audience were among the most common in the early weeks of the paper. In the first letters column, the only other correspondence published was on the same topic – a list of '10 "Don't"s for Opera Goers'. Two days later a correspondent applauded the attention given to the subject:

> That such remarks should appear so early in your paper seems to me a testimony of your future value. (3 April 1919)

The Opera House was clearly an important place of entertainment for the Army. According to the official history of the occupation, blocks of seats were reserved for the British, 'according to German custom', at prices ranging from the equivalent of two shillings to a few pence.

> The G.O.C. entered the opera house escorted by military police with revolvers in their hands, and no one was allowed to leave his seat until the general had left his box.[60]

It would not be unexpected that entertainment would be a topic of concern for young men with very little to occupy their free time in a foreign land. The first issue of the paper included a column advertising a range of entertainments in three army cinemas and two theatres. But that correspondence about the opera should have dominated the Letter Box might suggest an editorial bias towards the concerns of officers, rather than those of the men under their command (the first was signed 'Major'). But a letter (from 'J. O.') suggests a wider community of interest in the art form. The writer complained that officers were getting preferential treatment at the box office, while 'other ranks' were rudely turned away.

> There are many lovers of Grand Opera among the 'other ranks' in the army, and they would like something done to prevent the Opera House in Cologne (a public place of amusement) being reserved exclusively for Officers. (6 April 1919)

One hundred years later – and with only the published letters as evidence – there is no way of knowing whether the early emphasis on goings-on at the opera house accurately represented the contents of the editor's post bag. Apart from what he chose to print, the only other evidence of his policy is to be found in occasional references in the Cologne Post's own statements.

Bad behaviour at the Opera House did not only cause friction within the British community, it could also be seen as 'letting the side down', failing – in Baden-Powell's words – to be 'an example to the people in the midst of which you live'.

In the first letter published, about behaviour at the opera, it was not only the annoying habits of his fellow-officers that concerned the writer. He also referred to relations with the occupied population.

> Another view of the matter is that it lets us down very badly in the eyes of the Germans, who whatever else they may or may not be, are a musical people, and know how to behave at the Opera, which is more, apparently, than a large number of Englishmen know. (1 April 1919)

Relations between the British and the Germans went to the heart of the debate about community values. In the early days of the occupation, all contact between British soldiers and the German population was forbidden. 'A Maimed Officer' wrote to express his disgust at fraternization between British soldiers and Germans who less than 12 months earlier 'were torturing our prisoners, bayonetting our wounded'.

> When one is tempted to fraternize would it not be

only just and right to catch a glimpse in one's mind of the hundreds of thousands of wooden crosses which dot the lonely battlefields, and realize that although the war has mellowed in the background there are countless numbers whose lives will never be the same to them again. (28 September 1919)

It was relations with German women in particular which provoked the strongest feelings expressed in the letters column. On 29 September 1919, the editor's leader noted that 'in our correspondence columns the everlasting subject of women has been unquestionably the topic most fruitful of discussion ...'

This topic merits close examination, not only because of its quantity, but for what it says about the British in Cologne and the role of their newspaper in exploring and articulating their values.

Within days of the Peace Treaty (in June 1919) the paper carried an announcement of the engagement of two British officers to German women, which provoked a correspondent to ask (1 July 1919): 'Are mixed marriages between Englishmen and German women desirable from a national point of view?' 'An Englishman' was more outspoken (8 July 1919): 'It seems impossible to me that any man who has ever been in the firing line, could ever dream of it.'

Later in the year, there was a heated exchange of letters on the question of entertaining German women in British military clubs. By this time, some officers wives had moved to Cologne:

> We who have wives, feel it a great privilege to be able to entertain them at the Club, and feel sure that they in their turn do not desire that this privilege should be extended to the women of the nation we have so recently been fighting. (27 September 1919)

The writer was supported by a fellow officer:

> The brazen impudence of these German females is only equalled by the lack of feeling and tact shown by their escorts. (28 September 1919)

This was an example of a case where the paper followed up an issue raised by correspondents. On the front page on 28 September it carried a report of its investigation of the question and the assertion (from the officer in charge of the VI Corps Club) that there was 'absolutely no truth' in the allegation that German women were allowed in – though he did admit that one 'suspect' may have got away with it, thanks to her impeccable English.

It was not only the officers' clubs which attracted controversy. A report that the officer in charge of the Young Men's Christian Association club in Riehl (a suburb of Cologne) had prevented German children entering to watch film shows was welcomed by one correspondent. 'W. W.' had a clear idea of the difference in values between the Germans and the British community represented by the officer in charge of the YMCA:

Well, here's jolly good luck to him and more strength to his elbow; or if needs be to his fist. We need a place out here where we can take our wives and children for an evening's entertainment without fear of meeting with Germans ... I would like to see the Officer i/c extend his activities to soldiers who persist in bringing their 'frauleins' either into the pictures or on the verandah outside, in fact anywhere on the premises. I would suggest that all British women wear their brassard [identifying badge] conspicuously when visiting the Y.M.C.A. so as to help the work of complete exclusion of the Germans from a place that stands for Christianity and Justice and not 'Kultur and brute force'. (9 June 1920)

If anyone responded to remind the writer of Christ's injunction to 'suffer the little children to come unto me', their letter was not published. However, one reply suggested that 'W.W.' had built up a reputation among the Post's readers for a narrow-minded attitude to coexistence between the German and British communities:

Many of us who also have wives in Cologne are disgusted with the continual moaning of W. W. in your esteemed journal and elsewhere, and wonder if it is possible for him to live sociably with those (with) whom he comes into contact. (11 June 1920)

In the early days, the British on the Rhine were a predominantly male community and a strong strand of misogyny can be detected in the letters column. According to 'Dago', the conversation of the women of Cologne was one of the burdens the occupying army had to bear:

> Are Germans noisy? Gather four of the female variety together yapping and the nearest approach to the effect of the combination is the preliminary of a party of English terriers at the approach of a rat week ... I suppose so long as we have to occupy the Rhineland, we must put up with it. But it gets on my nerves and is injuring my ear drums. (23 October 1919)

German women may have been too loud for some, but the attention they received from other servicemen also annoyed one of the female members of the occupying forces:

> As an English girl who was at the Military Tattoo the other night when the deluge of rain suddenly overwhelmed us all, I was not too pleased to see how our soldiers attended to the wants of the German girls by bestowing their coats and waterproofs on fräuleins with whom they were probably hitherto unacquainted. There were many of their own countrywomen who were just as unprepared to face the elements. Gallant, our boys' conduct may have been; but many British girls went home sick at heart because of being neglected, as well as soaked to the skin. (10 August 1919)

Quite early on, soldiers returning from leave in Britain complained about the attitude of civilians – especially women - towards veterans of the war. There was a sense that community values were breaking down.

> I would like to know if any of our readers can fathom why we are treated with cold disdain by many of our own girls when on leave at home? To me it does not seem a wonder that so many of our Tommies prefer French, Belgian or – may I say it? – even German girls; after the way that the English girls have grown towards those who have been out here for their sakes and the homeland for four weary years? (8 July 1919)

> During my stay, (at home) I saw girls drinking and dancing with 'Aussies'. I was looked upon as dirt, and from several of my "demobbed" chums came the same story. One cannot relish the idea of returning home to make one of these 'left off's' his wife. (17 July 1919).

On the other hand, in 'A Final Batch of Letters on an Engrossing Subject' (including the previous one), there were those who spoke up for the 'English girl':

> A large majority of French girls I have met haven't a leg to stand on when compared with the average English girl. (17 July 1919).

> I have had plenty of experience with English, French and Belgian girls and a fair amount with fräuleins, but I can safely say that the English girl is superior to the others. (17 July 1919).

Once the peace treaty was signed, pressure mounted for officers' wives to be allowed to join their husbands on the Rhine. As early as April 1919, the paper published a letter referring to officers (not 'other ranks') who had served at the front and not seen their wives for five years. Among his arguments in favour of bringing wives to Cologne was to 'raise the moral tone of our Army'.

> The man who suggests that an Army quartered in an enemy country without the influence of its own womenfolk, is moral, is a fool. It isn't, and it is certainly not the case with ours. (10 April 1919)

Later in the year (18 July 1919), a reader was asking why only married women should be able to come to Cologne from Britain. 'Unmarried English girls' should be encouraged to make the trip – 'How else will Tommy find a wife?'

Once the officers wives began to arrive, the Post responded with a section of the paper targeting this new, female readership – 'Vanity Fair'. This was another example of the paper's clear focus on sales and potential audience, but it came as a shock to at least one 'Mere Man', who could feel an unwelcome change in the community on the Rhine:

> Up to then I had always looked on the 'Post' as being purely a man's paper .... I can't help feeling that many of the old school of soldiers must be a little pained at the new order of things and sigh for the good old

Army days, when man ruled supreme, and such innovation would have been unthought of. (6 September 1919)

The target audience did not agree, or at least one of them. 'Officer's Wife' replied:

There are a considerable number (of women) now in the Rhineland and to give them at least a corner in the 'Cologne Post' is I think nothing more than their due. (9 September 1919)

The arrival of their wives may have brought comfort to married officers, but not all their colleagues welcomed the women. 'Bachelor' questioned the effect on his fellow-officers' performance of their military duties:

It is a very pleasant thing, no doubt, to have one's wife and family on the Rhine. It makes one feel almost at home. But does it make for efficiency? … It's time off for this excursion or that entertainment; wifey must be taken to this sight or that; must go to the cafes and restaurants and have a good time generally. And hubby – well his work suffers. (14 Sept 1919)

In a series of replies, 'Bachelor' was described as 'a spiteful old thing', suffering from 'sour grapes'. One correspondent said the wives were not to blame for the fact that life among the garrison was dominated by a 'rush for pleasure and amusement':

> We live in a constant whirl of gadding about – theatres, opera, concerts, dances, not to mention music halls, variety concerts etc. (25 September 1919)

But 'One of the Married' (women) responded by invoking the spirit of sacrifice to which soldiers had referred in previous correspondence:

> Does 'Bachelor' give a thought to the four years of misery of the wives and mothers, who in some case (my own for one) have lost her sons in the way. Should she not have a little pleasure now? (16 September 1919)

In a leader column, the Post noted that news of the debate about 'efficiency' in Cologne had reached the pages of the Daily Mail and other papers in Britain, and issued a stinging rebuke to 'Bachelor' and his like.

> It is inevitable that the voice of the croaker must ever be heard in the land, but his grievance concerning the wife on the Rhine is ungenerous, unmanly, and uncalled for. Let him find another windmill, or if necessary another petticoat, at which to tilt. (24 September 1919)

Again and again, letters to the editor explored the limits of acceptable – and accepted – behaviour in the community. Not only were women 'over here', some of them wanted to take up sports traditionally played by men. Signing himself 'Pro Patria', an outraged writer predicted that the sins of the mothers would be visited on the children:

> I note with horror and disgust the ever-increasing tendency of our present day women to take up sports hitherto entirely devoted to the sterner sex. What must the result be? The de-sexing of the nation. What does this mean? It means the lowering in physique and morals of the fairest women in the world. The standard hitherto attained by the British women is such that they have been regarded as a model to all the women of the world. What do we see now? Women in scanty attire playing football, a game for which they are not physically suited. This will react on the next generation in a manner more terrible than one cares to imagine. (13 June 1920)

Perhaps only one thing could be worse – at least in the eyes of one correspondent from South Africa serving in the Imperial Army – the 'degrading spectacle' of a white woman dancing with a black man:

> I am not particularly prudish and I think I take a fairly broad-minded view of things in general, but I must admit I received a shock yesterday when I saw a native (a South African Kaffir I judged him to be) as the dancing partner of an English girl at the Deutsches Theater. (22 April 1919)

They may have been dancing to 'jazz', something which disturbed a fellow colonial officer ('Soul-less Rhodesia'):

> The performance I had the horror of witnessing, last Saturday, after a hard week's work, reminded me of the natives of Rhodesia in the Matoppos when executing their dances at their beer drinking festivities. (22 February 1920)

A question of race was the subject of the last letter published by the Cologne Post. It focused on a matter of intense controversy between the occupying allies and a Germany beginning to reassert its independence - allegations against black French colonial soldiers serving with the army of occupation. This was the 'black horror on the Rhine' ('schwarze Schmach am Rhein')

> Schwarze Schmach propaganda centered on highly graphic depictions of alleged sexual crimes committed by African soldiers against Rhenish women and children. The rape of 'innocent German maidens' by African 'barbarians' functioned as a metaphor for Germany's 'brutal subjection' under the Versailles Treaty and was aimed to deflect attention away from the debate over German war crimes. [61]

R. G. Coulson, in his memoir of four years in the occupation, recalled the anger of a German baron, who, in 1924, claimed that 'African savages swagger about in our streets and run after our women'.[62] 'The Post's coverage of this controversy was praised in a letter, headed 'The "Black Horror" Myth'. It came from a senior representative of the French Army of the Rhine.

> It was with deep satisfaction that I read your article, headed as above, in the 'Cologne Post' dated June 17th, in which you vindicate the honour of the black troops who comprise part of the French army of occupation, and which Army I am, at the moment, proud to serve. (23 June 1921)

That was the last letter published in the paper, but the intensity of correspondence appears to have declined throughout 1920 and 1921, no doubt linked to the great reduction in the number of troops (and families) in the garrison.

This review of the contents of the Editor's Letter Box does not claim to be comprehensive – and does not represent the full range of subjects covered. It has focused on issues which went to the heart of the discussion between the members of this unique community of English-speakers planted on the banks of the Rhine in a period of turmoil and uncertainty in Germany and beyond. Their concerns – at least as represented in these letters – may seem parochial. But they are a window on a society which fashioned 'a knowledge of itself', through the pages of its paper.

8. 'The Greater Game'

Sport in the Rhineland and the pages of the Post

The British Army had long believed in the centrality of sport in training for battle and, as it marched into the Rhineland, sought to deploy it as a foundation of peacetime occupation - a process in which the Cologne Post marched alongside in a crucial role.

The Army's apparent obsession with sport, and faith in its combat-training role, had long been a fact of not just military but civilian life. The Royal Engineers' team, for example, played in four FA Cup Finals in the 1870s (and won one – against the Old Etonians in 1875).[63]

By the time the First World War started, the role of sport in army life was so intense that it attracted ridicule from the Frankfurter Zeitung, which reported that: 'the young Britons prefer to exercise their long limbs on the football ground rather than to expose them to any sort of risk in the service of their country'.[64] The Army responded with a poster saying: 'Young men of Britain the Germans said you were not in earnest... Give them the lie – play the greater game'.[65] A century later The Greater Game, that is war itself, became the title of a book and an exhibition based upon it, at the National

Football Museum.[66]

By the end of the war the Army Sport Control Board, established in 1918, had become the regulatory body for all army sports and in 1919[67] the British Expeditionary Force Sports Board was created in France to coordinate divisional Sports Associations. The same year, the Army moved its Physical Training headquarters to Cologne, under the command of Lt Col J B Betts. Its instructors ran courses, trained more instructors, organised competitive sports, and even ventured into its own publishing, producing from 1920 lists of successes in a booklet called the Army Physical Training Staff Records, which began to carry longer features and evolved into a journal called Mind, Body and Spirit which by 1939 was carrying a cover picture of a perfectly formed young man in nothing but shorts, holding a flexed sabre.[68]

While one might argue over how appropriate football and cricket were to prepare soldiers for the Greater Game of trench-based slaughter, the Army knew that sport played an equal if not larger part when there was no fighting to be done. The National Army Museum explains that 'keeping troops occupied and out of trouble was an ongoing problem for the authorities. Eager to distract men from drink and prostitutes, senior officers recommended a range of sporting activities'.[69] There was also a fear of serious dissent, perhaps inspired by Bolshevism. 'It would be hardly too much to say that for one brief spell in February [1919] events hovered perilously nigh to open mutiny and partial dissolution of the force.'[70]

As the war drew to a close, therefore, the imperative to keep the men busy became more acute and in the occupied Rhineland 'the most elaborate schemes were formulated for sporting activities, the most popular of which was soccer.'[71] According to Tuohy,[72] cricket pitches and tennis courts were made wherever flat land could be found; Cologne's swimming baths were put to sporting use; a great annual swimming gala was held at Poll, on the Rhine; an 18-hole golf course was built at Rodenkirchen; and a Cologne gymkhana club was established, on the Merheim race course, with five meetings a year.

It was the Post that helped facilitate this. Over the past 40 years, a new mass market popular journalistic culture had been identified and the Post's own journalism reflected that. This culture, which was identified in the 1880s under the sweeping banner of 'the New Journalism', had in the space of a generation seen newspapers extend their remit beyond a narrowly political one to coverage of all aspects of daily life – including music, fashion, shopping, entertainment, recreation and of course sport. Indeed, the Daily Mail, which did more than any other British newspaper to shape the journalism of the 20th century was launched in 1896 partly off the back of its owner Alfred Harmsworth's success with a cycling magazine. Separate sporting publications, such as the Athletic News, had gathered readers in the same era and continued to prosper,[73] but sports coverage was now firmly part of the mass market press whether in Fleet Street or its Cologne outpost.

The New Journalism was not without its critics, and sports coverage has remained subject to some suspicion from those interested in journalism's allegedly higher functions. There was a late Victorian backlash against innovations such as personalized interviews, striking headlines, human interest stories and entertainment (in which one could include sport). It had been hoped that the combination of increased literacy and cheap press would provide the opportunity to educate and raise up the increasingly enfranchised masses. But the reality seemed that journalism was becoming what one would now call 'dumbed down'. The debate has continued ever since, with the tension between serious news, and sheer entertainment (including sport) 'part of a broader struggle between moral instruction and popular amusement'.[74] Criticism of sports coverage, in particular, continued indeed into the 20th and 21st centuries, with its practitioners allegedly inhabiting the 'toy department' of journalism where they produce distracting and inconsequential matter which displaces serious news.

The Post's ample coverage was, on the other hand, a fulfilling of journalism's other function. That is, not simply the transmission of information but the facilitating of ritual which helps bond communities[75] and indeed helps readers to imagine themselves as part of a community in the first place.[76] Sports coverage, along with other 'lighter' content about the reality of daily lives, was in this analysis not a dumbing down but a constructive, positive, celebration and validation of lives as they were really lived – a bolstering of popular rather than elite culture.

Debates aside, sports coverage was a daily fixture in newspapers by 1919 and with the Army's acute sense of what sport could do for their particular community, the Post's sporting relationship with its readers was set.

The paper 'gave them not only political news of the first importance, but the latest sporting news of every kind' according to William Le Crerar,[77] and Tuohy wrote that 'the CP always went all out on sport, giving pages to the Rhine Army and home events'.[78]

Going 'all out' meant that the Post was about one quarter sport: that is, out of the four large broadsheet pages that made up the daily editions of its early years, one was invariably given over mostly or entirely to sport. The mix was British Army of the Rhine (BAOR) and UK (home) sport, with sometimes a dash of international sporting news. For example in June 1919 it was routinely carrying lists of cricket fixtures (as many as 40) in the Cologne Post Cup competition covering four different leagues, plus reports and results; alongside a piece about the regulation of horses eligible to race in the occupied area; Rhineland racing tips; local cricket reports; and equestrian coverage, namely jumping and tent-pegging. It mixed this granular local coverage with for example, reports of a marathon from Windsor to London, open only to those who had served in the war, and won by a machine gunner; reports from home of an air derby; English country cricket, horse racing, polo, tennis, boxing (and rugby and football depending on the season).

By September 1919 the Post had also launched 'our

football competition', that is, a pools system which involved predicting soccer results on a coupon that readers could cut out and send in to the paper.

There were further sports ephemera, in for example the column called 'Answers to Correspondents' (which was also the title of another of Harmsworth's early magazines) in which around half of the subject matter, set by those who wrote in with a query, was frequently devoted to sport. For example, the column could variously confirm that in 1915 Sheffield United beat Chelsea 3-0; and that the fastest swimmer of the English Channel was Captain Webb, taking 21 hours and 45 minutes in 1875; but it was flummoxed by another query and replied 'we have no record of any such cycling achievement performed under the conditions you mention'. Sport brought in advertising, too, such as through the display advertisement for the Cologne Races, '1st enclosure and grand stand officers, 2nd enclosure and stand NCOs and men, ladies in uniform free', thus helping also to police the hierarchical boundaries of occupation life.

The reports themselves were detailed, analytical, authoritative, and somewhat prone as were sports reporters on the home newspapers to a breathless excitement which helped to convey the sense of live action.

In 1921 the Post was running its Upper Silesian Edition for troops based there and vowed on June 17 to 'include the full report of cricket, racing and all sports' because 'just a few English papers arrive here two or three days after publication ... hence the mass of the force is left without outside news'.[79] It reminded its readers, in the same editorial, that they were 'of every type and shade, and the policies immediately surrounding us, in such large and varied quantities, are no business of ours.' Sport was the glue that bound people in friendly competition, and perhaps distracted them from the divisive potential of politics.

The Post carried a lengthy piece in November 1919 about the urgent need for organised sports, headlined 'Critic hits out in defence of young soldiers'.[80] It was part of a chain of correspondence about the difference between the 1914-18 troops, who were now almost entirely demobilised, and those who had been sent to replace them. The former, it seemed, had a healthy enthusiasm for sport but their successors were less skilled, less fit, and less interested. All they needed, it seemed, was a more professional level of organisation to galvanise them.

The Post did not just report on sport, but helped make sport happen by offering its own trophies. In August 1919, for example, it ran the page three headline 'FOUR WEEKS TO GO. CPC Competition Reaching Its Culminating Stage', reminding readers that 'within the space of another four weeks all the teams on the leagues of The Cologne Post Cup Competition will have to complete their fixtures. Many outstanding matches remain still un-played, and secretaries must expedite matters as time is obviously limited. Until the league positions are decided, the competition cannot reach its culminating stage'.[81]

It was far from a neutral observer when it came to reporting on BAOR sports, and could be as partisan as any at home, for example when on Monday 1 August 1921, on page four, it carried the headline 'Inter Allied Sports Contests BRITISH BEAT FRENCH AT FOOTBALL', and said the 6-0 win would have been twice that if the ground had been softer. (The match was, incidentally, refereed by Captain Orlani of the Italian Army.)[82]

The Post's sports coverage remained undiminished during the later years of the occupation, despite the shrinking size of the garrison and the shift from daily to bi-weekly newspaper production. Rhineland coverage gave way somewhat to home coverage as the number of BAOR fixtures dropped, but the primacy of sport seemed to grow, with the subject increasingly likely to adorn or even lead the front page.

On Sundays in the later 1920s UK soccer results and other sport could occupy an entire column of what was by then a three column tabloid front page; and on 1 August 1926 almost all of page one was sport, with the lead story being the Highland Games (from home) plus English cricket alongside smaller items about a channel swim abandoned and BAOR cricket cancellations.[83] As a sign, perhaps, of the maturing position of the garrison and the Post itself in occupied Rhineland the newspaper published a tri-lingual horse racing supplement on Sunday 2 May 1926 – the Wiesbaden Racing Special, four pages split equally between text in English, German and French.[84]

The centrality of sport in occupation culture was so profound that the Post found itself not just reporting, organising, discussing, but leading too. This was particularly so when three sport-related reports in the home press denigrated the BAOR, and drove the paper to stand up for its readers as vigorously as any newspaper back home would have done for theirs.

Each incident took place in 1929, as follows.

The first was when the Daily Express ran a report alleging that Britons had been playing the enemy (that is, the Germans) at sport. Specifically, that 'the teams formed out of our army of occupation have met German teams time and time again in all sorts of sport, and nobody cared a button which side won, as long as the game was cleanly and stoutly played'. This, said the Post on 2 January 1929, under a report headlined 'Where Are The Facts?', was a gross libel on the BAOR.

> We challenge the Daily Express to publish details of the encounters ... we unhesitatingly deny that any representative of the British Army of the Rhine team has ever faced any German team ... time and again German sporting authorities have approached the British Army of the Rhine authorities with a view to games, especially soccer games, being fixed up. The reply has invariably taken the form of a polite refusal.[85]

The Post conceded that there had been a couple of private contests, between champion golfers and tennis players on each side, and that the German Mounted Police was once included in the jumping programme for the Army Horse Show, but this was a far cry from the repeated soccer matches alleged by the Express.

In February of the same year the British press was at it again, this time with the Daily Mirror claiming the BAOR had been playing the Germans at hockey. Not so, said the Post, taking the opportunity to revisit its robust rebuttal of the Express's allegations. Then, in September, the Post went into action for the third time, to correct the John Bull magazine which had produced a photograph of a BAOR soldier 'fraternizing' with a German woman. False, said the Post: 'That Tommy is staff sergeant Felgate, one of the BAOR's finest goalkeepers who happens to hold the record for appearances, and the woman he is talking to is his (English) wife'.[86]

The scale of the task for the Post, and the apparent professionalism at the way it was carried out, were hinted at in the farewell edition of the newspaper ten years later. BAOR soccer teams had toured Belgium, France, Luxembourg, and Czechoslovakia playing other British and allied military sides. Their prowess was matched by that of the Post's soccer correspondent, writing under the byline 'Tynesider', who was allegedly known the world over for his expertise and could only now be unveiled as Post journalist W. Le Crerar.[87] An entire page was devoted to capturing, in immense detail, the way the paper had reported on sports for the past decade. And, from a century's distance, its sports journalism comes across as well-researched, analytical, authoritative, and no more prone than other newspapers of the time to indulge in that tone of breathless excitement required to convey the sense of live action.

With its reporting of sport, the Post behaved not like a parish pump magazine covering the antics of obscure teams. Rather, it found itself at the centre of the mass market journalism of the time, providing that blend of hard and soft news, information and entertainment, that characterised not just the popular press but also the emerging BBC with its mission to inform, educate and entertain. And it is with the paper's sports journalism – from the results and reports to its wider facilitating role in the community – that one can perhaps best see where how (and how well) the newspaper adapted the norms and practices of contemporary journalism within the constraints of its unusual position in the grey area between the army and its soldiers.

9. Informing, Educating & Entertaining

The Cologne Post and the development of British journalism

The great British Colony in Rhineland, both Military and Civilian, look to the Cologne Post *daily to bring them first news from home and exclusive news of Rhineland, Sport, education, amusement…*[88]

This chapter pulls together many of the themes discussed so far and places them in the wider context of the development of British journalism after the Great War.

The newspaper press had by 1919 experienced some forty years of the 'New Journalism', that popularisation of journalism for the mass markets that emerged from the 1880s.[89] Improvements in literacy, the growth of accessible urban readerships, the increased harnessing of communications technology to printing, news gathering, and distribution – all these had presented a new opportunity for editors and proprietors. They seized them with gusto, expanding the remit of journalism beyond politics and into the daily, social, lived lives of their readers in pursuit of previously unimaginable sales and advertising revenue. Interviews, lively headlines, human interest stories, sport, fashion, and lifestyle features became commonplace in the new mass market popular press which at the launch of the Post was little more than a generation old.

Launches tell the story: that of the Daily Mail in 1896, the Express in 1900, and the Mirror in 1903. By 1921 the Mail was selling 1.5m a day, the Mirror a million, the Sketch 835,000, and the combined sales of the Express, Chronicle, Herald and the News amounted to more than another million. That the Cologne Post should so wholeheartedly adopt for its broad readership key elements of this popular form of journalism, rather than the staid variety that persisted alongside (e.g. the Times), should not therefore surprise us. But the Post's context was significantly different from that of, for example, the Mail, Express, or News of the World.

Popular newspapers might articulate, and even follow, 'public service' ambitions such as truth-telling, holding power to account, community-building and campaigning. The newspapers of Harmsworth and similar publishers not only campaigned and crusaded but contained 'a strong flavour of self-improvement' which is evident in the Cologne Post too. However, private ownership and commercial imperatives produced media which served and created distinct markets (some local, some national, some narrow, some broad) in order to gain circulation and advertising revenue. Newspapers had to 'give the readers what they want', mirror the concerns and prejudices of their audience, mould their readers' attitudes and in some cases feed their fears and reinforce their prejudices – in the process creating a 'virtuous' circle for the business. Policy was then and now decided by commercial owners and their editors, based on personal whim or assessment of the most effective business strategy.[90]

Against the background of competition for mass readership there developed a discourse about the lowering of standards, the pandering to appetites for sensationalism, sleaze, and the presentation of news as entertainment. From the beginnings of the New Journalism in the 1880s and into the 20th century and beyond the popular press was itself routinely held to account for its squandering of opportunities to educate and inform the masses. The dream of a burgeoning press helping to civilize the emerging masses had not been wholly realised. According to Ferris the legacy of Harmsworth, for example, was that 'what looked like vices – expediency, glibness, prejudice – were virtues in the new Fleet Street.'[91]

In a striking comment on the state of the press, Norman Angell gave evidence to the Sykes committee on the future of broadcasting, which reported in 1923. He had worked for eight years on Northcliffe's Daily Mail and believed a reformed popular press could be 'a means of creating a reasoned, reasonable public opinion':

> If any progress ... was to be made against the prevailing disorders of the public mind, that mind had to be reached largely through the Press. How could this be

done? How could sense and rationalism be made as attractive as the Hearsts and Harmondsworths seemed to make nonsense and irrationalism?[92]

Publication of the Sykes Report was one of the important milestones in the development of the concept of 'public service' in relation to what would now be called the media. It was wireless, not a reformed press, which strove to create the 'reasoned, reasonable public opinion' that Angell had wished for. That was the basis of John Reith's vision of a 'public service', which would rise above the commercial concerns which had created the press landscape of the early 20th century.

'News, education, amusement' – those key words in the Post's promotion of itself (quoted at the head of the chapter) are reminiscent of the editorial values which became the watchword of the BBC, founded like the newspaper in the wake of the Great War. It is John Reith, its first Director General, who is generally given the credit for creating this new approach in the 1920s, with his aim of 'informing, educating and entertaining' the audience.[93] But as early as 1919, the Cologne Post was aspiring to a similar idea of public service.

John Reith successfully transformed a commercial company, aimed at creating a market for wireless, into a public corporation, established by the state but maintaining a degree of independence even at a time of national emergency. Free from competition, the BBC could pursue its high-minded mission to inform, educate and entertain.

Reith shared with many of the pioneers of radio in the BBC a personal experience of war, through service in the armed forces. David Hendy in particular has researched the influence and resonance of the Great War on the early BBC and its approach to broadcasting – to an audience which had also been impacted by the greatest conflict in human history.

Both the Post and the BBC were established in the years following an unprecedented conflict, in a world in which new values were emerging - including collectivism, the extension of the franchise, the emancipation of women, and the rise of organised Labour. Key figures in both organisations shared a common experience as soldiers, which influenced their attitude to the postwar world. The newspaper and the broadcaster both existed in a condition of semi-independence from the state. Neither was driven by the profit motive. For both, the idea of 'impartiality' was central. Most importantly, they both had a concept of their audience as an inclusive community. And both developed their journalism – in the broadest meaning of the word – in reaction to the development of the popular press over the previous 40 years.

Despite the differences between these two media, in scale, location, delivery, and duration, there are many areas where a comparison can throw a light on the development of journalistic values and approaches in the years after 1918.

At the BBC, Reith's vision of public service would depend above all on its freedom from the need to make money.

> Although it had been brought into existence by a combination of manufacturing interests, such 'elements of commercialism' as had been evident in the early days of the company had disappeared. ... It is interesting to note that Reith gave prior attention to this facet of broadcasting as a public service – its lack of dependence on the profit motive.[94]

The Cologne Post's freedom to follow a 'public service' path in its journalism was equally dependent on its lack of commercialism. There is ample evidence that the paper was run in a business-like way, working to maximise its circulation, its appeal and its advertising revenue. But it is equally clear that making a profit for shareholders was not a driver. As it stated in a leader:

> The Cologne Post does not ... attempt to be a money-making concern. It has no desire to earn dividends. It is content if in its role of daily journal for the Rhine Army it pays its way.[95]

Financial security, free from the profit motive, was closely linked with editorial independence. But freedom from commercial pressure was not in itself a guarantee of editorial independence, either in the case of the Cologne Post or the BBC. Each had to negotiate its relationship with the state and its constituent parts.

Chapter one described the Cologne Post's 'world scoop'

and its boast that although closely connected to the British State – to the Army on active service – it had published the terms of the treaty in defiance of an order to delay, in the interests of its readers.

The Post made no bones about its link to the military. The strapline on the first issue spelled out its relationship with the state: 'A Daily Paper published by the Army of the Rhine'. It made no overt claim to independence and acknowledged the limitations on the subjects it could discuss (specifically anything in breach of King's Regulations). In the final issue of 1929, it described itself as 'a semi-official organ'. It is significant (as has been seen) that, when questions were asked in the House of Commons in May 1919, the Secretary of State for War (Winston Churchill) said the paper was 'under the control of the General Officer Commanding of the Army of the Rhine'. But six years later, his successor told MPs that it was not an official publication 'except in so far as the military authorities exercise a control over its contents'.[96]

The status of the Cologne Post was not so different from that of the BBC a few years later. 'The position of the Corporation is ... one of independence in the day-to-day management of its business, and of ultimate control by His Majesty's Government'.[97] The ultimate power of the Government over the BBC was revealed in September 1939, when – at the outbreak of the Second World War – the Corporation was immediately put under the 'general command' of the new Ministry of Information.[98]

Looking back to the BBC's early years, the Ullswater Report quoted the Postmaster General in 1926:

'While I am prepared to take the responsibility for broad issues of policy, on minor issues and measures of domestic policy and matters of day to day control, I want to leave things to the free judgement of the Corporation.'[99]

The 'second facet' of Reith's vision of public service broadcasting was that it 'could and should serve everybody in the community who wished to listen'.[100]

According to the Cologne Post (looking back, in its final edition in 1929), 'the business side' of the publishing adventure was not a primary concern for the 'small band of experienced journalists' drawn from the ranks of the occupying army, who saw 'the unparalleled scope for such a publication.'

The great appeal to them lay in that the newspaper would be an asset of great value to Great Britain, and a guide and a friend to the men, sharing their troubles and pleasures, and stimulating them to the full consciousness of their positions.[101]

The idea of 'public service' depended on a clear sense of who the public was. Newspapers segmented the market, creating and nurturing a readership in their own image. For the Cologne Post, with no competition, and no need – or desire – to narrow its appeal, the audience were the English-speakers in the Rhineland. At first, these were almost all soldiers and almost all men; later a more diverse English-speaking colony developed in Cologne and the paper adapted to serve it.

Although the Post's potential audience could be defined clearly in general terms, it could not be said to be homogeneous. Just like British society, it was divided by class and by regional or national identity. As it asked in an early editorial, 'Was there ever a newspaper issued to a heterogeneous public in circumstances comparable to ours?'[102] The Cologne Post had to form a concept of the 'community' it aimed to serve, as did the BBC.

Reith envisioned radio as an unparalleled means of bringing into being a new kind of public – an 'imagined community', in Benedict Anderson's phrase, whose collective consciousness would be as listeners with a sure sense of national identity grounded in a shared moral understanding.[103]

In a very real sense, the British on the Rhine – as seen by the Cologne Post - were 'an imagined community'. The 'Watch on the Rhine' was underpinned by a set of shared values, apparently understood and occasionally articulated. In an early leader column previously mentioned, under the heading 'Citizen Soldiers', the Post expressed its conception of a readership with which it closely identified:

> We are really a British colony of British citizens who are showing a defeated enemy the ideals which inspired us in the war and which are still untar-

nished.[104]

One particular way in which the Post created a sense of its community was through the letters column which it published during its first, formative year (see chapter 7). There its readers raised issues of common concern and debated the correct answers to questions such as the correct relationship with the occupied Germans (male and female) or acceptable behaviour in the Opera House.

Reference has been made to how Wahl-Jorgensen (quoting Habermas) describes the letters section as 'one of the few places where "society as a whole fashions a knowledge of itself" – a place where members of diverse groups can gather for a shared conversation about the issues that concern them all.'[105] So it certainly was in the columns of the Cologne Post.

The idea of public service enshrined a set of values which were clearly based on a mission to improve and uplift. The Cologne Post identified itself with a British civilising mission in Germany. As has been shown, its coverage highlighted cases where the British authorities upheld the values of law and order in the occupied territories, as in the case of the British military judge who criticised people in Cologne for failing to obey the rules of the road for pedestrians and motorists, concluding that 'there is too much of this Bolshevism about in these days'.[106]

John Reith would have applauded the judge and the attention paid to his comments by the paper. Burns sees the BBC between the wars as 'instinct with the kind of cultural and moral zeal which was Reith's own personal endowment to broadcasting'.[107] According to Avery, Reith saw broadcasting 'as a vehicle of national discipline'.

> Drawing on his understanding of Matthew Arnold's cultural theory, he conceptualized culture itself and the new cultural form, broadcasting, as allies in a fight against 'doing as one likes', one of Arnold's definitions of anarchy.[108]

In its early days the Cologne Post was unashamed in preaching, in its leader column, a mission for the British on the Rhine as 'Missionaries of Empire', with the power to create a 'new view' of Imperial Britain 'which has not always been regarded, even by peoples in alliance with us, as a fair, righteous creation of noble, disinterested statesmanship'. The story of 'the Soldier on the Rhine' – supported by his paper – might prove to be 'the greatest chapter in Britain's military history'.

> Let the Army of the Rhine 'play the game'; let it 'play the man', all day and every day … we keep our watch on the Rhine to carry out the policy of our leaders and by carrying out that policy we can give flesh and blood to what shall make for a better and nobler world. There lies our responsibility, and it is only proper that The Cologne Post should put the matter thus early before its growing mass of readers.[109]

Impartiality, balance, fairness have become watchwords associated with the BBC and widely contrasted with the values of the printed press. Reith saw his public service broadcasting system acting 'as a dependable keeper of the nation's conscience', standing as 'an arbiter above the clamour of all political and social factions' and regarded as 'the paragon of impartiality, honesty and respectability'.[110]

The Cologne Post accepted the restrictions on the topics on which it could comment – much as the BBC, in its early years, was obliged to avoid coverage of 'controversial' topics. The Post made a virtue of its politically neutral position.

> There is much good work to be done by an efficient and dignified army newspaper. First of all, it can supply to soldier exiles the news of the world from which they are shut off, and it can supply news well in advance of the arrival of home papers. If it is a disadvantage that full comments must not be made on all items of information it certainly is an advantage to have news that is not garbed in any propagandist fashion.[111]

A striking example of the paper's commitment to impartial and balanced journalism can be seen in its front page coverage of a national rail strike in Britain in October 1919. Within its main report on the dispute is a paragraph quoting the Secretary of the Railwaymens' Union and his complaint that 'the newspapers are not reporting his version of the men's case in full'. Alongside, under the heading 'Pros and Cons of the Dispute', the Post (in contrast to the papers complained of) set out first the 'Railwaymen's Case' and then the 'Government's case' – 'in order that our readers may grasp the actual points of the dispute'.[112]

The paper was proud of its editorial standards and not afraid to criticise journalists who failed to live up to them – whether in Germany or at home. As has been seen, it criticised the Daily Express for 'a gross libel on the British Army of the Rhine', after it claimed soldiers were playing football with Germans. And it hit out at a local paper, The Maerkische Zeitung for publishing false accounts of disturbances in Cologne: 'It is difficult to understand why any newspaper, even of the most scurrilous type, should resort to such contemptible inventions.'[113]

The preceding pages have highlighted areas where the Cologne Post revealed a commitment to several pillars of what became known as public service journalism. One other important factor in common with the early BBC was the background of the Great War itself.

David Hendy's research on the BBC places an emphasis on the influence of the war, and the shared experience in the armed forces of many of the founding members of its staff, which was 'stuffed full of ex-military types', starting with Reith and including a long list of others.

> War had touched an entire generation. And it was this generation of men and women who helped set up the BBC in 1922 or joined it soon after in key posi-

tions.[114]

Hendy notes, for example that Lance Sieveking, the early BBC producer, was frequently addressed as Captain Sieveking, while at work.[115]

The Cologne Post, of course, was a direct product of the war, founded to serve a military readership at a time when hostilities had been suspended, not ended. It is perhaps not surprising that an army of 275,000 men should include a handful with experience of journalism and the enthusiasm to launch a new publication despite the practical obstacles in their way. For ten years they sustained a unique newspaper in occupied territory. When it was all over, some of them joined the staff of the BBC.[116]

Map of the occupied Rhineland 1919

References

Anderson, B. 2006. *Imagined Communities, Reflections on the Origin and Spread of Nationalism*. London: Verso.

'Apex' (Coulson R. G.) 1931. *The Uneasy Triangle – Four Years of the Occupation*. London: John Murray.

Avery, T. 2006. *Radio Modernism, Literature, Ethics, and the BBC, 1922-1938*. Aldershot: Ashgate.

Barnhurst, K.G. & Nerone, J. 2002. *The form of news: A history*. New York: Guilford Press.

Bogdanovic, N. 2017. *Fit to fight: a history of the Royal Army Physical Training Corps 1860-2015*. London: Bloomsbury

Bourne, R. 2015. *Lords of Fleet Street: The Harmsworth Dynasty*. London: Routledge.

Bownes, D. & Fleming, R. 2014. *Posters of the First World War*. London: Bloomsbury.

Briggs, A. 1961. *The History of Broadcasting in the United Kingdom, Vol 1*. Oxford: Oxford University Press.

Bundesarchiv (German Federal Archives) https://commons.wikimedia.org/wiki/File:Bundesarchiv_Bild_146-1971-091-20,_Kapp-Putsch,_Marine-Brigade_Erhardt.jpg

Burns, T. 1977. *The BBC, Public Institution and Private World*. London: Macmillan.

Cain, J. 1992.*The BBC, 70 Years of Broadcasting*. London:

BBC, 1992.

Cain, P. J. 2012. Character, 'Ordered Liberty', and the Mission to Civilise: British Moral Justification of Empire, 1870–1914 in *Journal of Imperial and Commonwealth History*, Vol. 40, No. 4, November 2012, (pp. 557–578).

Carey, J.W. 2008. Communication as culture, revised edition: *Essays on media and society*. London: Routledge.

Chalaby, J. 1896. Northcliffe: proprietor as journalist. In Catterall, P. et al (eds.). 2000. *Northcliffe's legacy: Aspects of the British popular press, 1896-1996*. London: Palgrave Macmillan.

Edmonds, James. 1944 (reprinted 1987). *The Occupation of the Rhineland 1918-1929*. London: HMSO.

Evans, R. J. 2003. *The Coming of the Third Reich*. London: Penguin/Allen Lane.

Ferris, P. 1971. *The House of Northcliffe: a biography of an empire*. New York: World Publishing Company.

Hansard, *House of Commons Debates* vol. 115, 1 May 1919; vol. 182, 24 March 1925.

Hendy, D. 2012. Biography and the emotions as a missing 'narrative' in media history, *Media History*, 18:3-4 (pp361-378).

Hendy, D. 2014. The Great War and British broadcasting: emotional life in the creation of the BBC, in *New Formations*, issue 82 (2014) 82-99.

Jackson, A. 2014. *The Greater Game: A history of football in World War I*. London: Shire Publications.

Keynes, J. M. 1920. *The Economic Consequences of the Peace*. London: Macmillan & Co.

MacMillan, M. 2001. *Peacemakers – The Paris Conference of 1919 and Its Attempt to End War*. London: John Murray

Markham, Violet R. 1920. *A Woman's Watch on the Rhine*. London: Hodder & Stoughton.

Monthly Notices of the Royal Astronomical Society. 1922. Vol. 82, p.253 http://adsabs.harvard.edu/full/1922MNRAS..82..253.

Nicholas S. 2007. Keeping the News British: the BBC, British United Press and Reuters in the 1930s, in *Wiener J.H., Hampton M. (eds) Anglo-American Media Interactions, 1850–2000*. London: Palgrave Macmillan.

Osborne, J. 1989. 'To keep the life of the nation on the old lines': The Athletic News and the First World War, in *Journal of Sport History* 14.

Pawley, M. 2007. *The Watch on the Rhine* London: I.B. Tauris

Radio Who's Who 1947 https://archive.org/stream/radiowhoswho00andr/radiowhoswho00andr_djvu.txt

Roos, J. 2015. Schwarze Schmach, in *Daniel et al. (eds) 1914-1918 Online - International Encyclopedia of the First World War*. Berlin: Freie Universität Berlin. https://encyclopedia.1914-1918-online.net/article/schwarze_schmach

Scannell, P & Cardiff D. 1991. *A Social History of British Broadcasting, Vol 1*. Oxford: Blackwell.

Tuohy, F. 1930. *Occupied 1918-1930, A Postscript to the Western Front*. London: Thornton Butterworth.

Wahl-Jorgensen, K. 2001. Letters to the Editor as a Forum for Public Deliberation: Modes of Publicity and Democratic Debate in *Critical Studies in Media Communication*, Vol. 18, No. 3 (pp. 303-320)

Wahl-Jorgensen, K. 2007. *Journalists and the public: newsroom culture, letters to the editor, and democracy*. Creskill, NJ: Hampton Press.

Ward, A. 2015. *A Guide to War Publications of the First & Second World War: From Training Guides to Propaganda Posters*. Barnsley: Pen and Sword

Watt, R. M. 1969. *The Kings Depart – The Tragedy of Germany: Versailles and the German Revolution*. London: Weidenfeld & Nicholson

Wiener, Joel H., ed. 1988. *Papers for the Millions: the New Journalism in Britain, 1850s to 1914*. New York: Greenwood Press.

Williams, K. 2009. *Read all about it! - A history of the British newspaper*. London: Routledge.

Williamson, D. G. 2017. *The British in Interwar Germany – The Reluctant Occupiers, 1918-30* London: Bloomsbury.

https://www.forces.net/news/who-were-only-military-team-win-fa-cup

https://www.nam.ac.uk/

Photographs

The Imperial War Museum has an extensive online collection of photographs of the occupation of the Rhineland, including several specifically relevant to the Cologne Post.

Machine room of the Kölnische Volkszeitung where the "Cologne Post", a daily paper published by the British Army of the Rhine, was printed. This machine was able to print 18 000 copies an hour. The manager and editor of the Kölnische Volkszeitung, can be seen in the left foreground. Cologne, 1919: http://www.iwm.org.uk/collections/item/object/205236262

Scene in the editorial room of the "Cologne Post", a daily paper published by the British Army of the Rhine. The first editor was William Edward Rolston (from 24 February 1919) and the first sub-editors were J. W. Nevill, E. T. Moore (from 25 February 1919) and E. Ingham (from 1 March 1919), possibly all present in the photograph. These were the entire British staff. Cologne, 1919: http://www.iwm.org.uk/collections/item/object/205236265

Troops of the Cheshire Regiment buying from a German woman the first number of the "Cologne Post", a daily paper published by the British Army of the Rhine. Photograph taken in the Old Town Square outside the Cathedral, Cologne, 1919: http://www.iwm.org.uk/collections/item/object/205236261

R. H. Hardy, the Advertisement Manager of the "Cologne Post", a daily paper published by the British Army of the Rhine, between 20 March and 15 December 1919. Cologne, 1919: http://www.iwm.org.uk/collections/item/object/205236263

Members of the Church Army Women's Theatre Company buying the first number of the "Cologne Post", a daily paper published by the British Army of the Rhine. Cologne, 1919: http://www.iwm.org.uk/collections/item/object/205236260

Two Germans, one of them a policeman, reading the peace terms [in the *Cologne Post*] outside a building in Cologne: http://www.iwm.org.uk/collections/item/object/205236375

About the authors

Rob Campbell graduated with a first class honours degree from Exeter University and became a newspaper reporter in Hertfordshire. His press career from then involved freelancing on national titles, and sub-editing and management roles on regional daily newspapers, for example as features editor on the Western Daily Press. He gained an MA in Mass Communications, and took two breaks out of journalism: one as an English teacher in Spain and Oman, and the other as a government press officer.

For the last ten years he has taught journalism at the University of South Wales. He completed a PhD on the subject: 'Harmsworth's daily timesaver, 1901: a transatlantic case study in the tabloidisation of reader time'.

James Stewart is a graduate of Cambridge University. He began his career in journalism on the South Wales Echo & Western Mail. He went on to work for the BBC as

Environment Correspondent and for ITV as editor and producer of current affairs. He has trained journalists in many parts of the world and joined the University of South Wales in 2008. From 2012 to 2019 he taught International Journalism at Cardiff University. His grandfather, Cpl. Evan Jenkin Kingsbury, served in the Army of the Rhine from December 1918 to December 1919.

Notes

[1] 'We published the Peace Terms at least eight hours ahead of the world's press', Cologne Post, 26 July 1919. See also Tuohy, 150ff.
[2] Tuohy, p.151
[3] Cologne Post 3 June 1928
[4] ibid. 31 March 1920
[5] Watt, pp. 399-412
[6] Cologne Post 31 March 1920
[7] Watt, p. 416
[8] Watt, p. 406
[9] MacMillan, p. 469
[10] Evans, p.72
[11] Cologne Post 3 Nov 1929
[12] ibid.
[13] Cologne Post 31 March 1919
[14] 'Bummeling': derived from the German word *bummeln*, meaning to stroll leisurely, usually in nature
[15] Cologne Post 3 January 1929
[16] Cologne Post 3 February 1929
[17] Hansard – 1 May 1919 (reply to Mr Bottomley)
[18] Hansard – 24 March 1925 (reply to Mr E. P. Nicholson)
[19] Such was the scale of British deployment at the time, including that of conscripted servicemen, that histories of the period overlap with personal and family his-

tories. For example, in 1919, three of the four grandfathers of this book's co-authors were bearing arms in the Rhineland, Afghanistan, and Ireland.

[20] Pawley, p.5

[21] Monthly Notices of the Royal Astronomical Society, Vol. 82, p.253 http://adsabs.harvard.edu/full/1922MNRAS..82..253.

[22] Where original source material uses abbreviations for ranks etc these are spelt out for clarity when appropriate. Thus, Sergt becomes Sergeant and L/Cpl Lance Corporal.

[23] Radio Who's Who 1947 https://archive.org/stream/radiowhoswho00andr/radiowhoswho00andr_djvu.txt

[24] Nicholas S. (2007) Keeping the News British: the BBC, British United Press and Reuters in the 1930s. In: Wiener J.H., Hampton M. (eds) Anglo-American Media Interactions, 1850–2000. Palgrave Macmillan, London.

[25] Ridgway went on to write a number of books and edited the Everyman's Encyclopedia.

[26] ProQuest: Trench Journals and Unit Magazines of the First World War

[27] Barnhurst & Nerone

[28] Evans, p.104

[29] In January 1922, the cover price of the *Cologne Post* had been 2 marks; by June that year it had risen to 500 marks, by 9 November 1923 it was 10,000 million marks. By February 1924, it had risen to 100 milliard (100,000 million) marks – but it could also be bought for just one British penny.

[30] British Military Memorandum of 27 November 1918; Edmonds, p64.
[31] Dr Josef Beckers, quoted in Williamson, D. The British in Interwar Germany.
[32] Cain, p. 560
[33] Edmonds, p84.
[34] Konrad Adenauer, later Chancellor of the Bundesrepublik
[35] Williamson, p34.
[36] Pawley, p.119
[37] 'Apex', p.200
[38] Hansard, House of Commons Debates vol. 115, 1 May 1919
[39] It is interesting to note that six years later, when another (unrelated) question was raised in the house about the *Post*, the then Secretary of State for War replied that the paper was not financed from Army funds and was not an official publication 'except in so far as the military authorities exercise a control over its contents'. (Hansard, House of Commons Debates vol. 182, 24 March 1925)
[40] 'Apex', pp. 58-60
[41] Williamson, p.135
[42] 'Apex', pp.49-50
[43] Williamson, p.222
[44] Sir Percival Phillips, cited by Tuohy, p. 218
[45] Tuohy, p. 220
[46] Bundesarchiv Bild 146-1971-091-20
[47] Williamson, p. 159
[48] Tuohy, p. 220
[49] Markham, p.230

[50] 'APEX', p. 7
[51] Williamson, pp.134-136
[52] 'Uncle Ebenezer' is reminiscent of the 'uncles' and 'aunts' who presented Children's Hour on the early BBC. 'The first officers of the BBC both in London and the provinces had to reconcile themselves to becoming 'uncles' and 'aunts', with all that this meant, not only in the eyes of children, but to some extent at least in the eyes of the public as a whole. Uncle Arthur, Uncle Caractacus, Uncle Leslie, Uncle Jeff, Uncle Rex, Uncle Humpty Dumpty, Uncle Jack Frost, and Aunts Sophie and Phyllis became household names in the course of 1923.' (Briggs, 260)
[53] 19 shillings and 11 pence was one penny short of a pound, also known as a sovereign.
[54] Wahl-Jorgensen (2007), p.3
[55] Kapoor & Botan (1992) quoted in Wahl-Jorgensen (2007), p.3
[56] Cologne Post 3 November 1929
[57] It is striking, in the context of the readership of a newspaper targeted at an isolated linguistic community, that Anderson emphasizes the role of printing in creating a sense of a linguistic community or nation. (Anderson (2006) 37-46)
[58] Wahl-Jorgensen (2001), p.310
[59] Wahl-Jorgensen (2001), p.309
[60] Edmonds, p.118
[61] Roos, 2015
[62] 'Apex', p.60
[63] https://www.forces.net/news/who-were-only-military-team-win-fa-cup

[64] Bownes & Fleming p.58
[65] Ward p.24
[66] Jackson
[67] https://www.nam.ac.uk
[68] Bogdanovic
[69] https://www.nam.ac.uk/
[70] Tuohy, p.37
[71] Williamson, p.17
[72] Tuohy
[73] Osborne
[74] Williams, p.12.
[75] Anderson
[76] Ibid. pp 150-152
[77] Cologne Post, 3 November 1929
[78] Tuohy
[79] Cologne Post (Upper Silesian edition), 17 June 1921
[80] 16 November 1919
[81] August 1919
[82] 1 August 1921
[83] 1 August 1926
[84] 2 May 1926
[85] 2 January 1929
[86] 8 September 1929
[87] 3 November 1929
[88] Cologne Post, 27 September 1919 (emphasis added)
[89] Wiener, 1988 / Joel H., ed. *Papers for the Millions: the New Journalism in Britain, 1850s to 1914*. New York: Greenwood Press, 1988.
[90] Among British newspapers, the only exception is the Guardian, owned by the Scott Trust, which was formed in 1936 'to secure the financial and editorial independ-

ence of the Guardian in perpetuity and to safeguard the journalistic freedom and liberal values of the Guardian free from commercial or political interference'.

[91] Ferris, p309

[92] The Broadcasting Committee Report (The Sykes Report) (HMSO, London, 1923) cited in Scannell & Cardiff, p6.

[93] It was not Reith but David Sarnoff, an early pioneer of radio in the USA, who first combined the three words which came to symbolize the BBC's public service mission. In June 1922 he argued that 'broadcasting represents a job of entertaining, informing and educating the nation, and should therefore be distinctly regarded as a public service'. (Briggs, 59 – see detailed citation).

[94] Briggs, p235

[95] Cologne Post, 2 October 1919

[96] Hansard, 1 May 1919 and 24 March 1925 (emphasis added).

[97] Ullswater Report, 1936; cited in Burns, p12

[98] Burns, p21

[99] ibid.

[100] Briggs, p236

[101] Cologne Post, 3 November 1929

[102] Cologne Post, 25 April 1919

[103] Avery, p15

[104] Cologne Post, 1 August 1919

[105] Wahl-Jorgensen, p3

[106] Cologne Post, 2 April 1924

[107] Burns, p36

[108] Avery, p15

[109] Cologne Post, 8 April 1919

[110] Burns, p155
[111] Editorial, Cologne Post, 25 April 1919
[112] Cologne Post, 1 October 1919
[113] Cologne Post, 6 July 1922
[114] Hendy (2012), p373
[115] Hendy (2014), p96. See also Burns 16ff; Scannell & Cardiff, p6.
[116] During the Second World War Harry Maule-Ffinch, who had worked on the Cologne Post joined the BBC Overseas News Division, becoming English Editor, in charge of news and programmes transmitted to Europe in English.

Printed in Great Britain
by Amazon